AF320497

Meiry Maria Guimarães
Rosângela Lopes Borges
Valéria F. D. Carvalho

The educator, play and the teaching-learning process

Meiry Maria Guimarães
Rosângela Lopes Borges
Valéria F. D. Carvalho

The educator, play and the teaching-learning process

Case study in an Early Childhood Education Centre

ScienciaScripts

Imprint

Any brand names and product names mentioned in this book are subject to trademark, brand or patent protection and are trademarks or registered trademarks of their respective holders. The use of brand names, product names, common names, trade names, product descriptions etc. even without a particular marking in this work is in no way to be construed to mean that such names may be regarded as unrestricted in respect of trademark and brand protection legislation and could thus be used by anyone.

Cover image: www.ingimage.com

This book is a translation from the original published under ISBN 978-613-9-73116-9.

Publisher:
Sciencia Scripts
is a trademark of
Dodo Books Indian Ocean Ltd. and OmniScriptum S.R.L publishing group

120 High Road, East Finchley, London, N2 9ED, United Kingdom
Str. Armeneasca 28/1, office 1, Chisinau MD-2012, Republic of Moldova, Europe
Printed at: see last page
ISBN: 978-620-7-89585-4

Copyright © Meiry Maria Guimarães, Rosângela Lopes Borges, Valéria F. D. Carvalho
Copyright © 2024 Dodo Books Indian Ocean Ltd. and OmniScriptum S.R.L publishing group

MEIRY MARIA GUIMARÃES

Degree in Pedagogy (UEG, 2003); Postgraduate Diploma in Teaching Methods and Techniques (UEG, 2003); Specialisation in Early Childhood Education (APOGUEU, 2010); Master's Degree in Educational Sciences (MARIA SERRANA, 2017); PhD student in Educational Sciences (DEL SOL).

meirymariaguimaraes@gmail.com

ROSÂNGELA LOPES BORGES

Graduated in Languages (Port./Ing.) (UEG, 2006); Postgraduate in Special Education (POGEU, 2010); LIBRAS interpreter (ASG, 2011); Specialisation in Clinical and Institutional Psychopedagogy (UNINTER, 2017); Master's student in Professional and Technological Education (IFGoiano). She is currently a university lecturer and part of the Multidisciplinary Team of the Specialised Psychopedagogical Care Centre - NAPE, at the Caldas Novas College, in the state of Goiás, Brazil.

rosalb2@hotmail.com

VALÉRIA FERREIRA DIAS CARVALHO

Degree in Pedagogy (UNIP, 2017); Postgraduate course in Clinical and Institutional Psychopedagogy (2018).

valeriaferreiradiascarvalho@gmail.com

INDICE

INTRODUCTION

The world's economic, social, educational, cultural and political transformations favour the evolution of people's thinking, and this is no different with children. Technological developments have brought about an environment that is no longer the same as before. The learning methodologies of traditionalist education have undergone significant changes, because it is necessary to offer children a more fruitful school childhood.

The school should be a great partner for teachers when they are willing to look for new ways of teaching, other than the traditional ones. It should give everyone, students and teachers alike, the chance to try something new. Learning must be meaningful and enjoyable for the child who is beginning their new role as a student.

The author's concern arose from questions related to the teacher's training and attitude, since it is the role of this teaching agent to define the choice and use of school materials, how to plan the arrangement of objects in the classroom environment, and also the activities that will be carried out.

The first aspect to emphasise is that playful activities are not restricted to games and play, but include activities that enable moments of pleasure, surrender and integration for those involved. These are activities that provide an experience of fulfilment, in which students are fully involved, flexible to learning and healthy.

In play activities, what matters is not just the practice of the activity, or what results from it, but the action itself, the moment experienced. It allows those who experience it to have moments of encounters with themselves and with others, moments of fantasy and reality, of resignification and perception, moments of self-knowledge and knowledge of others, of looking after oneself and looking at others, moments of life, of expressiveness.

This work is justified by the operational importance of working with play in cognition or improving children's cognitive development. The aim is, among other things, to show how playfulness as a whole can contribute to the cognitive, physical, social and emotional development of pre-school children; to analyse the pedagogical functions of playfulness as a necessary aid to children's development; and to show how playfulness can be included in an organised way in the school context.

The aim of this study is to: investigate the use of play as a tool for the teaching-learning process of students, by Early Childhood Education teachers; observe the importance of play for the teaching-learning process of Early Childhood Education students; investigate whether teachers have made use of playful tools to teach their students; and analyse the perception that teachers and students have regarding playful pedagogical practices.

The first question to be asked is: What influence do the games and games used by nursery school teachers have on the teaching-learning process? Another judgement to be answered is how playfulness has been used in the pedagogical practice of Early Childhood Education, whether it is respecting the natural character of the child, since each of them has peculiar preferences related to their age?

We present the hypotheses that we intend to clarify at the end of this research project, which was carried out in order to contribute to improvements in the educational field. There is a presumption that early childhood education teachers do not have any specific training in the area of play, either as a subject during their undergraduate or postgraduate studies, or as a continuing or refresher training course. As a result, they have only used play to fill the children's time and keep them occupied during their stay at the institution.

As a theoretical reference, the research was based on studies carried out in the field of literary critical theory, which came from reading authors who defended the use of play in the classroom as part of the teaching-learning process: Kischimoto (1993) and Ferreira (2000). The theories of Vygotsky (2007) were also fundamental to the conclusion of this work because, in his work studied, the author draws parallels between the positive and negative aspects of using play, opening up a new space for dialogue.

This study is structured into five chapters, which are described as follows:

The first chapter, Protocol Framework, describes the work in general terms. It includes a description of the problem; the generic and secondary research questions; the general and specific objectives; the justification; the delimitation and limitation of the topic.

The second chapter, Theoretical Framework, describes the basic concepts surrounding the subject; the historical context of play; its use in Early Childhood Education; pedagogical practices; new technologies; play in stories; the teaching-learning process; the role of toys in child development; the importance of methodology; constructivism; teachers and their training.

The third chapter, Methodological Framework, will cover the approach; the type of research; the time and space delimitation; the population; the sampling and inclusion criteria; the hypothesis; the data collection techniques and instruments; the primary and secondary sources of information; the ethical conditions and how the collected data will be processed.

In the fourth chapter, Analytical Framework: this section aims to present the observations made, as well as analysing the data from the survey with the teachers and the students' parents. In addition, the observation data will be analysed.

In the fifth chapter, the aim is to set out the final considerations and recommendations that emerged after analysing the data.

Finally, the bibliographical references of the theoretical framework will be presented, as well as the appendices created to carry out the field research.

CHAPTER 1

PROTOCOL MILESTONE

1.1 DESCRIPTION OF THE PROBLEM

Playful activities include playing, toys, games, dances, theatre, storytelling and music. Nursery rhymes, old games and guessing games are also considered playful activities. Playfulness is the practice of these activities within schools, as pedagogical practices used in the teaching-learning process.

Carneiro (1995) emphasises that everyone has an inherent culture of play, just like children. It is therefore understood that this culture is produced by individuals all the time and consequently changes as society itself changes.

It is known that the teaching-learning process becomes more enjoyable and more efficient if it is carried out through games, play and dance. This is because these activities are innate in children. Antunes (2005) believes that children learn more, more quickly and retain the content they are taught when it is transmitted through playful activities.

Given the importance of playful activities for the teaching and learning process of children in early childhood education, the question arises as to whether teachers are prepared to use them in the classroom. It also asks how children respond to the stimulus of playfulness and which playful activities are being used by these teachers and whether they have achieved any results.

1.2 RESEARCH QUESTIONS
1.2.1 GENERAL QUESTIONS

What influence do the games and plays used by teachers at Early Childhood Centres have on the teaching-learning process?

1.2.2 SECONDARY QUESTIONS

Have the teachers at the Early Childhood Centres used play as a tool to teach their students?
What is play and how can it improve children's performance at school?
What do teachers and students think about play as a mechanism for teaching?

1.3 RESEARCH OBJECTIVES
1.3.1 GENERAL OBJECTIVE

To verify the use of play as a tool for the teaching-learning process of the students, by the teachers of the Early Childhood Education Centres.

1.3.2 SPECIFIC OBJECTIVES

Observing the importance of play for the teaching-learning process of the students at the Early Childhood Centres.

To investigate whether teachers have used playful tools to teach their students.
To analyse teachers' and students' perceptions of playful pedagogical practices.

1.4 BACKGROUND

This study is justified by the importance that play plays in the teaching-learning process of students at Early Childhood Centres. Almeida (1995) defines playful education as an action that is inherent in children and is always linked to knowledge and collective thinking.

Sneyders (1996) explains that education is about moving towards joy. For him, play techniques enable children to learn with pleasure, joy and entertainment. In order to do this, the naïve idea that play is just a pastime or a superficial diversion must be abandoned.

The aim of this work is to conceptualise play and demonstrate its importance in child development. To understand playfulness in education as a methodology that brings more pleasure and meaning to the teaching-learning process. It is understood to be a powerful mechanism for stimulating social life and the constructive development of children in early childhood education.

1.5 DELIMITATION AND LIMITATION

The aim is to conduct a survey of teachers, parents and pupils at the CEI - Centro de Educação Infantil (Early Childhood Education Centre) in order to understand how play is used in the teaching-learning process of these children.

The instruments used in this study will be obtained in the municipality of Caldas Novas, Goiás, Brazil. Specifically in the Municipal Early Childhood Education Centre of the municipal education network, called the Pequeno Príncipe Early Childhood Education Centre.

In this context, there is free access to the educational institution because the CEI in question is where the author of this project works. It is understood that as she is a teacher at this educational institution, she will have easier access to the data that will be compiled and investigated.

CHAPTER 2

THEORETICAL FRAMEWORK

2.1 CONCEPTUAL FRAMEWORK

Early Childhood Education: Early Childhood Education is the phase involving children aged 0 to 6, considered the first stage of Basic Education. Its objective is the integral development of children, i.e. not only cognitive, but also physical and socio-emotional.

Play: A way of developing creativity and knowledge through games, music and dance. The aim is to educate, teach, have fun and interact with others.

Teaching and learning: For him and many contemporary educators, educating someone is a dialogical process, a constant exchange. In this relationship, educator and learner exchange roles all the time: the learner learns while teaching their educator, and the educator teaches and learns from their student.

2.2 HISTORIC MILESTONE

From a historical point of view, the upbringing of children was the exclusive responsibility of the family for centuries, because it was in socialising with adults and other children that they took part in traditions and learnt the norms and rules of their culture.

From a historical point of view, it took almost a century for children's right to education to be guaranteed in legislation, and it was only with the 1988 Constitutional Charter that this right was effectively recognised.

Two years after the approval of the 1988 Federal Constitution, the Statute of Children and Adolescents - Law 8.069/90 - was approved, which, by regulating Article 227 of the Federal Constitution, inserted children into the world of human rights. In the following years, from 1994 to 1996, the Ministry of Education published a series of important documents entitled "National Policy for Early Childhood Education". These documents established pedagogical and human resources guidelines with the aim of expanding the supply of places and improving the quality of care at this level of education.

In today's society, on the other hand, children have the opportunity to attend a socialising environment (crèches and CMEIs), living together and learning about their culture through different interactions with their peers.

For Didonet (2001), talking about crèches or early childhood education is much more than talking about an institution, its qualities and defects, its social need or its educational importance. For him, it's talking about the child. A human being, small, imperceptible, but alive and important for future society.

2.2.1 THE HISTORICAL CONTEXT OF PLAY

The word "ludic" has its origins in the Latin word *'dudss'*, which means "games" and "play". And this play includes games, toys and fun, and scholars believe that this helps the individual's learning. The inclusion of play in schoolchildren's lives is a very effective way of penetrating children's worlds in order to pass on knowledge (ALMEIDA, 2006).

According to Santos (1997, p. 23), "The toy, understood as an object that supports play, presupposes an intimate relationship with the child, their level of development and indeterminacy in terms of use, i.e. the absence of a system of rules that organises its use." It is understood that if the student maximises and develops their creative side, their learning will be more effective and the teacher's wishes will be met.

It's not known for sure when it all began, but the history of play in Brazil begins with the arrival of the colonisers[1] , in indigenous lands. Along with them came other cultures, team and individual games and evangelisation and teaching (KISHIMOTO, 1993).

The same author adds that the indigenous people, even if they didn't know it, taught their children traditional labour in a fun and enjoyable way, and the children absorbed what they were taught. The response to the parents' efforts to pass on their knowledge to their children was a positive learning result.

Baldus (1970) apud Kishimoto (1993) states that although the effort to preserve the historical collection of toys made by certain ethnic groups has been safeguarded, modernity is destroying this memory because toys are becoming increasingly sophisticated. This means that children no longer value toys as they used to.

Children's games of yesteryear mark a time when children created innocent stories, drew their favourite characters, used what they had in their environment to invent a way of having fun (ALMEIDA, 1995). Learning was something natural and inherent to children who were often shredded by their surroundings. Games such as "Vendinha" and "Casinha" were the reproduction of adult life, in the form of games, where you learnt by playing.

In the past, the cries heard in the streets at dusk were cries of joy and life, reproduced through games such as: "Pega-Pega", "O Chefe Mandou", "Cabra-cega", "Caí no Poço", "Bete" and others. Each of these games had an intrinsic sense of learning (ALMEIDA, 1995).

Nowadays, you no longer hear the euphoric cries of children in the street, because they are locked up in their homes working on a computer (KISCHIMOTO, 1993). Not to mention the fact that many lose the desire to go to school, because educational institutions, unfortunately, offer a canned, bank study, full of rules and duties (FREIRE, 1987).

Curto (2000), in his book "How children learn and how teachers can teach them to write and read", argues that teachers must realise that teaching has changed. They must realise that teaching methods must be the drivers of learning that is focused on what the student needs to learn and not just on what the teacher wants to teach.

The aforementioned author also argues that teachers, with a few exceptions, still don't accept innovations in the educational environment, especially when it comes to teaching methodology for children. For him, teachers must realise that the time when children went to school simply to play without any commitment to learning is over. What we see today are schools based on a commitment to teaching and, above all, realising that children learn much more through play.

Play is part of human behaviour and has been present throughout human history as part of the culture of all societies. Each with its own specific cultural symbolism. Children have always used and still use play as a form of socialisation. From the point of view of Cultural Anthropology, play takes on different connotations depending on the socio-cultural context (MACEDO; PETTY; PASSOS, 2005).

According to Ferreira (2000, p. 37), play is "[...] a way of developing creativity and knowledge through games, music and dance. The aim is to educate, teach, have fun and interact with others." In other words, all the games that involve teaching and learning can be considered playful tools for learning and teaching.

In order to understand how it is necessary to use play as a learning tool, we need to understand its genesis as a cultural experience. Winnicott's (1995) concept of the transitional object is fundamental to this, as the influence of the environment is decisive in the psychic development of human beings.

According to the theories of this British paediatrician and psychoanalyst, children who are still babies use certain soft objects or toys to release all the tensions and conflicts that permeate their mother's short absences. This happens even before the weaning period. These objects are called

---

1 The colonisation of Brazil took place at the end of the 15th century, in the year 1500, when some European nations were involved in maritime-commercial expansion. At that time, nations such as Portugal and Spain set out in search of new sea routes and new lands, locating new lands to the south of the American continent (Brazil) in the 1500s.

transitional because they occupy an intermediate space between internal and external reality.

> This transitional space persists throughout life. It will be occupied by extremely varied
> playful and creative activities. Its function will be to relieve the human being of the constant
> tension caused by the relationship between the reality within and the reality without (NASIO,
> 1995, p. 194).

The imaginary is interconnected with play in the psychic process, and in this respect Vygotsky (2007) states that:

> To resolve this tension, the child enters an imaginary, illusory world in which desires are
> unattainable: this world is what we call play. Imagination is a new psychological process for
> the child, in other words, it is not present in the consciousness of children (VYGOTSKY,
> 2007, p. 121).

Following the author's reasoning, children from the age of two reproduce themselves in everyday or role-playing games. These imaginary situations are not necessarily symbolic actions. The basic meaning of playfulness is to learn the rules of morality and local culture.

According to Aragão and Silva (2010, p.3), there is a danger that the game will take on a purely random character when misused. This can happen when students, for example, play and try to get motivated by the game alone, without understanding the educational meaning embedded in the game. According to the authors, this happens when the educator doesn't have mastery of the subject or "[...] specific training in this area that many consider insignificant, but which is of great value to those who know it."

For Piaget (1975), the evolutionary phases of play in school emerge gradually as the child moves from infancy to pre-school. At first, children are more focussed on the real objects they use when they play. Later, they focus on objects as social interaction and begin to develop more complex games, with various functions and symbolic uses.

Bergen (2002, p. 35) calls the child's repetition phase at pre-school age "[...] Repetitive, unimaginative play". This is because many children at this age have not yet developed cognitive skills and stick to the imitation method. His research states that as children grow older, they tend to spend less time playing and more time on sports and/or virtual games.

The big problem with this shift in focus is that in these activities (sports and virtual games), children have to follow the rules, and rarely have the opportunity to discuss, negotiate or change their norms. For the author, this is an extremely important skill that contributes to the development of social competence and self-regulation[2] (BERGEN, 2002).

When they learn to play, it follows its natural course and is based on the function of play, they start to enjoy themselves because they are no longer stuck memorising the rules. Children are given an opportunity to develop and apply their social and self-regulation skills. When play is completely replaced only by sports or other organised activities, these important skills may not develop fully (MACHADO; FRISON, 2012).

According to Bergen (2002) it is in pre-school that children have the opportunity to get to know play and learn while playing. Some studies show that when children are properly supported in their play, play doesn't get in the way of learning; on the contrary, it contributes to it.

Most educators, in search of concrete results, leave play out of the school curriculum, or use it in their free time. The curriculum cannot be seen as a mere content tool (GARCIA, 2003).

Piaget (1975) and Vygotsky (2007) were the first researchers to relate play to cognitive development. The effects of play on learning and development have currently been of great interest to scholars of child development and learning.

In a global analysis of the numerous studies on play, researchers have found evidence that play contributes to advances in verbalisation, language, vocabulary, comprehension, attention,

---

[2] The property of something or someone that regulates itself without external action. 3. establishment or verification of rules made by the person or entity being regulated at the time.

imagination, concentration, impulse control, curiosity, problem-solving strategies, empathy, cooperation and group participation (MACEDO; PETTY; PASSOS, 2005).

2.3 THE USE OF PLAY AND EARLY CHILDHOOD EDUCATION

Nowadays, technology is advancing rapidly in various sectors, including education. That's why activities involving playfulness can't be forgotten and relegated to the background in everyday classroom life.

The insertion of a playful instrument as a way of teaching, if applied correctly, can be very rewarding. According to Fischinger (1970, p. 75), "the lack of space or time to play can lead to possible developmental disorders. By playing, children develop their creative spirit."

Lopes (2006) also shares this idea:

> Play is one of the fundamental activities for developing identity and autonomy. The fact that children can communicate with gestures and sounds from an early age, and later act out certain roles in play, helps them to develop their imagination. Through play, children can develop important skills such as attention, imitation, memory and imagination. They also develop some socialisation skills through interaction, using and experimenting with rules and social roles (LOPES, 2006, p.110).

We can see that children's contact with toys makes learning more natural and enjoyable, as toys are the way they understand the world they live in. According to Oliveira (1989), this is an opportunity to develop, because it is through play that children move, experience, discover and create. As a result, they acquire experiences that lead to sociability and the ability to take initiatives and decisions on their own.

According to Ronca (1989), play allows children to explore the relationship between their bodies and space, creates possibilities for movement and speed, and provides the mental conditions to get out of trouble. It is through these conditions that they develop psychomotor and affective skills, and broaden concepts in the various areas of science. Play therefore becomes a pleasurable source of knowledge.

Csikszentmihaly (1997) argues that the state of mind influences the ability to concentrate and absorb what is being experienced. He calls it flow or a "state of self-forgetfulness", which occurs when people become so absorbed in what they are doing that they lose all awareness of themselves, forgetting about small problems. The author explains that flow happens in that delicate zone between boredom and anxiety.

When play takes place in situations where the needs are greater than the usual ideal, the result is more satisfactory for learning. The ideal stage of a game in learning is one that takes place in a delicate zone between boredom and anxiety, between what the child feels and what is happening at the moment. This means that the proposed game or play must offer excitement that is in tune with the individual's emotions (RONCA, 1989).

For Vygotsky (2007):

> Children form mental structures through the use of instruments and signs. Play, the creation of imaginary situations, arises from the tension between the individual and society. Play frees the child from the constraints of reality (VYGOTSKY, 2007, p. 84).

In a similar vein, Vygotsky (2007), Ronca (1989) and Csikszentmihaly (1997) argue that when children play, they are absent from themselves, it's a state of catharsis or flow in which they forget their conscience, their worries and tensions are abandoned. It is a creation of a liberated state.

Playful practices give children the opportunity to relate to their peers and experience the most varied sensations that are essential to them. Through play, children show how they see and construct the world, how they would like it to be (SOARES, 2001).

Knowing this, according to the aforementioned author, teachers need to rethink playfulness as a learning tool. This professional is then given the chance to address and realise this dynamic at the moment when lessons are planned.

Sneyders (1996 p.36) states that "Educating is moving towards joy". A life without joy becomes boring, monotonous and sad. Education is no different. Without playfulness, the teaching-learning process becomes uninteresting and discouraging. And that's bad for the teacher and even worse for the student. The author argues in his book "Happy Students" that the use of games and play throughout the pedagogical process is of fundamental importance so that content can be taught in a pleasant and engaging way.

Further emphasising the importance of play, Ronca (1989) states that:

> Play allows the child to explore the relationship between the body and space, provokes possibilities of movement and speed, or creates mental conditions to get out of trouble, and they assimilate and spend so much that this movement makes them seek out and experience different fundamental activities, not only in the process of developing their personality and character, but also throughout the construction of their cognitive organism (RONCA, 1989, p. 27).

According to the author, children get to know themselves and others through play,

recognises their limits and respects the limits of others, learns that there are rules for everything, including the simple act of playing, and that these are meant to be respected. Establishes behaviours related to habits and culture. Internalises, albeit superficially, the concepts of ethics and morality.

According to the 1998 National Curriculum Framework for Early Childhood Education:

> Make-believe games, construction games and those with rules, such as social games (also known as board games), traditional games, didactic games, body games, etc., encourage children to expand their knowledge through play (BRASIL, 1998, p. 28).

Based on these definitions, it is expected that play as a form of learning can develop the creative spirit, sharpen curiosity and work the imagination, allowing children to get involved and seek solutions to their questions and concerns.

Novaes (1992, p. 28) complements this idea by saying that "[...] Teaching, absorbed in a playful way, acquires a significant and effective aspect in the development of the child's intelligence.". This means that children understand more when they learn through play, becoming capable of assimilating learning into other daily contexts.

Given that play mobilises subjectivity, facilitating the development of the cognitive aspects of the child who plays, Santos (1997) sees the need for research into child development through play. The author believes that doing so will bring a greater possibility of transforming (for the better) the relationship between educator and student.

The same author, quoted above, warns that often, with the aim of transforming play into a useful activity, they lose their characteristic of freedom and come to be seen as uninteresting work. This leads to the game or play being completely removed from playfulness.

2.3.1 PLAY AND PEDAGOGICAL PRACTICES

Because of its importance, play is valid for all grades and not just for Early Childhood Education, as is commonly thought. Ronca (1989, p.99) says that *"[...] play, games and fantasy, as activities related only to childhood [...] are not restricted only to the world of children.".*

Sometimes teachers wonder how to teach a particular subject using play. Playful teaching is didactic and can be fun if the teacher knows how to use it. Leisure activities are attractive and motivating, they capture pupils' attention and encourage them to think, develop their language and search for game strategies (NOVAES, 1992).

The importance of games in emotional and cognitive interaction is clear, but the teacher must know how to use them at different times during the lesson. For example, when a child is apathetic or sleepy when some subject or content is being explained, the teacher can insert a game, a round-robin game or a game of divines. This shows the diversity of approaches that play can provide.

According to Mcedo, Petty and Passos (2005):

> The game is social by nature since its participants relate to each other and obey the same rules as their opponents, and the affective side is revealed in the mobilisation of emotions and energy. In the cognitive field, skills such as reasoning, anticipating moves and predicting the consequences of actions are emphasised (MACEDO; PETTY; PASSOS, 2005, p. 18).

The same authors specify that when teaching maths, the teacher has a thousand ways to go. Among the teaching strategies that can be used, the researchers argue that for children to learn how to make games, they initially need to have contact with a variety of them.

Antunes (2005) says that when children realise the different ways they can use games, they pay more attention to how they work and learn more quickly. For this to happen, the teacher needs to show them the cognitive possibilities. This means that the teacher must explain how the game works and what its purpose is.

Storytelling is also a playful activity which, according to Rodrigues (2009), provides children with the opportunity to enjoy a story:

> Storytelling is an activity that encourages imagination and the transit between the fictional and the real. When preparing a story to be told, we take the narrator's and each character's experience as our own and broaden our lived experience through the author's narrative. The facts, scenes and contexts are imaginary, but the feelings and emotions transcend fiction and materialise in real life (RODRIGUES, 2009, p. 4).

In relation to reading, Macedo, Petty and Passos (2005) say that children like to invent while they play. They invent friends, come up with strategies, tell stories, and it's at this point that the teacher should interact. They also emphasise that good writers are masters at inventing stories.

Thus, it can be inferred that when creating a story, whether fanciful or not, the child, in a communicative approach, feels the need to use language and specific vocabulary to give reality to the moment in which they are playing. This happens even when they don't yet know how to read, in which case the teacher, after the story, makes idagations that motivate the students to trigger the actions coherently. It's an opportunity to awaken an interest in reading and the ability to interpret (RODRIGUES, 2009).

According to Curto (2000), teacher/student interaction at reading time is of the utmost importance because it is on the school floor (in a circle) that we know what the child has learnt or not. The author also explains that the teacher must always be aware of what is happening in the classroom in order to know the right moment to introduce the play activity.

2.3.2 PLAY AND THE NEW TECHNOLOGIES

Another point we want to address is learning through new technologies. For children in early childhood education, the computer is a playful object. An object that most of them have access to at home.

For Castells (2006, p. 219) "The use of computers in education began in 1969 at the University of California, Los Angeles (UCLA)". For the author, *the* spread of the use of computers by universities brought a different perspective to education.

Playing with computers gives children access to new technologies, while at the same time placing them in a larger context, that of virtual globalisation. With the advance of technology, the ways of teaching have become interactive and children are perhaps the most proficient with computers and the *Internet*. The virtual game brings them closer to a fantastic world where they can even have their own *avatar*[3] (NASCIMENTO, 2012).

---

3 In computer science, they are created figures similar to the real player.

Also according to the author mentioned above, when children are doing something in the computer lab they feel much more at ease than in the classroom itself. We can therefore see the importance of keeping an educational institution's computer lab in favourable conditions for use.

It is known that not all schools offer this space (computer lab), but intervention projects should be created that focus on seeking donations from public or private organisations of at least ten computers for students to use (CASTELLS, 2006).

According to Nascimento (2012), games that require reasoning are very well received by children because they see them as challenges. They like to be challenged in their limitations, an example of which are maths games where they learn to add and subtract by playing.

The acts of play and games, even if they are not done intentionally, promote the development of the individual. Almeida (2006) says that teachers should recognise the importance of working with play and have the vision that it is another tool that can facilitate teaching and learning.

Libâneo (1994) argues that teaching practice requires analysing the here and now, one of the factors influencing the classroom, in order to identify the needs of each group and achieve student learning. For him, students need to learn to solve problems, critically analyse and transform reality in order to identify concepts, learn (to learn, to do and to be) and thus discover knowledge in a motivating and fun way.

In the classroom, we need to develop cognitive independence, an eagerness for knowledge and student protagonism, so that there is no fear in solving problems. The school's commitment is to form a confident, creative, motivated, strong and constructive man, capable of realising his potential, under the guidance of his teachers (GARCIA, 2003).

The objectives of education cannot be achieved by using explanatory and illustrative methods alone. We need to introduce innovative methods which, according to Perrenoud (2002), is the right way to raise the quality of education.

The main element of playful learning is the game, an educational resource that has been explored at all levels of education to enrich the teaching-learning process. Nascimento (2012) says that learning is enriched by the dynamic and virtual space of online games, which have the ability to transform the big into the small, the ugly into the beautiful, real things into imaginary ones, students into professionals.

2.3.3 The PLAYFULNESS OF TALES

In addition to new technologies as a pedagogical practice, teachers should look for other dimensions such as reading fairy tales. Curto (2000) warns that teachers' attitudes when it comes to reading will define the type of reader they want to train.

According to Almeida (2006), fairy tales fill children's reading and learning moments. And if this moment is well planned and approached with playful characteristics, it will become more enriching.

During reading, in this mixture of play and fantasy, the teacher can materialise the learning they had set out in the teaching plan. Curto (2000) argues that the introduction of fairy tales into children's school life is a very effective way of entering the child's universe to pass on knowledge and all the interaction of the adult universe.

According to Lajolo and Zilberman (1999) they should be used as a support for play:

> Fairy tales understood as an object, a support for play, presuppose an intimate relationship with the child, their level of development and indeterminacy in terms of use, in other words, the absence of a system of rules to organise their use (LAJOLO; ZILBERMAN, 1999, p. 23).

It is understood that if a child develops creatively in the school environment and manages to enhance their learning, they will certainly have absorbed the teacher's wishes, provided they are planned. A story should not be told simply for the sake of telling it or memorising it; it must have a purpose (VIEIRA, 2005).

It is known that teachers, with a few exceptions, still don't accept innovations in the educational system, especially when it comes to teaching children. Garcia (2003), however, points out that teachers must realise that teaching has changed, and along with it, the methodologies, practices and didactics used in the classroom.

Gone are the days when children went to school simply to play without any commitment to learning. Today we see schools based on a commitment to teaching and, above all, realising that children learn much more through play. Considering fairy tales as a strategy for children to invent their own stories, the aforementioned author sees the pleasure of "playing" as a learning tool.

By this, Freire (1987) means that adults conduct their learning in a direct and real way, while children need this "play-learning" in order to meet and socialise with the outside world.

We can therefore conclude that children should not be seen as alien to the world in which they live. Fairy tales educate them from the moment they do not escape their real world, but bring the stories they have read and enjoyed into their childhood world (ALMEIDA, 2006).

2.4 THE TEACHING-LEARNING PROCESS IN EARLY CHILDHOOD EDUCATION

Playing and learning are inherent to children. The fact that they play develops their perception and imagination, and this translates into school. This means that, if they are allowed to, they will use play as an instrument for their own learning, whereas adults use work as an object for learning, producing and reproducing (GARCIA, 2003).

In this comparison between the child's "play" and the adult's "work", we realise that through play the child is transported into the midst of the rules of coexistence that they will be expected to follow as an adult.

Freire (1987) explains:

> Adults produce and learn by working, children by playing. Children work and learn through play. It is through this that the child comes into contact with the world of rules. Every game has its rules that must be understood, incorporated and respected by the child (FREIRE 1987, p. 74).

In other words, the author means that adults lead their learning in a direct and real way. However, the child needs this, to play while learning, in order to meet and socialise with the outside world. Both actions occur automatically and instinctively.

For Vygotsky (2007), children should not be seen as alien to the world in which they live. The toy instructs them from the moment that they do not run away from their real world, but bring the playful activities that cause them pleasure into their childhood world. He also argues that proximal development[4] of the child, the closer the child gets to the toy, the more they learn, the greater the contact, the greater the apprehension.

The aforementioned author makes it clear that linking play and pleasure is risky, because there are much more pleasurable things for a child in the learning phase than the toy itself. When referring to this subject, Vygotsky (2007):

> Defining a toy as an activity that gives the child pleasure is incorrect for two reasons. Firstly, many activities give the child much more intense experiences of pleasure. Secondly, there are games in which the activity itself is not pleasurable (VYGOTSKY, 2007, p. 107).

---

[4] The Zone of Imminent Proximal Development (ZDI), a concept developed by Vygotsky, defines the distance between the current level of development, determined by the ability to solve a problem without help, and the range of possibilities, determined by solving a problem under the guidance of an adult or in collaboration with another partner.

Thus, according to the author, the teacher must be careful when exposing the child to play objects without at least allowing the child to have first contact with them. Each child will respond differently to this stimulus.

Piaget (1978, p.120-121) says that: "children's play is an assimilation of the real into the self", in other words, play is an activity that transforms the real, due to their affective and cognitive interests. In the teaching-learning process, contact with make-believe play allows children to create playful symbols that can function as a kind of inner language.

Vygotski (2007, p.75) says that "Play contains all the tendencies of development in a condensed form, and is itself a great source of development." Regarding the development of children's learning, Vygotski (2007, p.75) says that "Play contains all the tendencies of development in a condensed form, and is itself a great source of development.

When playing, the child starts on an imaginary level and always ends up transferring this imagination to a real situation. It is through play that children project their reality and let their imagination flow, thus creating opportunities to develop cognitive skills and releasing emotions (OLIVEIRA, 1989).

2.5 THE ROLE OF TOYS IN CHILD DEVELOPMENT

Toys are essential tools for the proper development of children. This is why Kischimoto (1995) argues that the playroom is the magical space created to give children the opportunity to play in an enriching way, to immerse themselves in their toys without the interference of adults.

Oliveira (1989) says that play plays an important role in the formation of concepts, skills, expectations and socialisation in children. Historically, children have always needed an activity; to move, navigate, manipulate objects and experience, to create, interact and exchange actions, experiences and feelings.

According to Benjamin (2002):

> When children use toys, in addition to combining heterogeneous materials (stone, sand, wood and paper), they make sophisticated constructions of reality and develop their creative potential, transforming the function of objects to fulfil their desires. Thus, a piece of wood can become a horse; with sand, they make cakes and sweets for their imaginary birthday party; and chairs become trains, in which they act as conductors, imitating adults (BENJAMIN, 2002, p. 76).

It can be seen that play is a key element in school education. Children learn while playing, so this activity becomes important for the child's learning. A school that makes use of play provides children with great benefits, including contributing to the development of cognitive potential, perception, the activation of memory and the language of the arts (SANTOS, 1997).

According to Kishimoto (1995), it's not just a matter of handing the child a toy. The structure of the classroom needs to be planned and systematic. This organisation ensures that students are more mobile and that their development becomes consistent and meaningful. This statement reveals the teacher's pedagogical commitment and professional training.

According to the definition in the Aurélio dictionary, the word "toy library" is an area reserved for toys in schools and nurseries (FERREIRA, 2000). ABBRI - Associação Brasileira de Brinquedotecas (Brazilian Toy Library Association), in order to emphasise that a toy library is not just an area reserved for toys, cites the 10 main objectives of a toy library on its online portal:
   a) Provide opportunities for children to play without demanding performance;
   b) Stimulate the development of the ability to focus attention and build a rich inner life;
   c) Stimulate the child's operativeness, thus favouring their emotional balance;
   d) Give opportunities for potential to emerge;
   e) Nurturing intelligence and creativity;
   f) Provide a greater number of experiences;
   g) Provide opportunities for them to learn to play, participate, wait their turn, compete and co-

operate;

h) Valuing emotional feelings and cultivating sensitivity;
i) To enrich the relationship between children and their families;
j) Encourage the valorisation of play as an activity that promotes intellectual and social development.

In the current context of Early Childhood Education, toys have two uses with different meanings: those that value the socialisation of children and therefore adopt free play, and those that adopt schooling and educational toys aimed at acquiring school content (GARCIA, 2003).

2.6 THE IMPORTANCE OF METHODOLOGY

The act of planning is part of human history, as the desire to turn dreams into objective reality is a major concern for everyone. One of the elements underpinning effective planning is the definition of content objectives, accompanied by the choice of the appropriate method for a given learning situation.

Ferreira (2000, p. 505) defines method as: "1. procedure, technique or means of doing something, esp. according to a plan. 2. organised, logical and systematic process of research, instruction, investigation, presentation, etc.". It is therefore understood that the method is important in order to achieve true knowledge of the objectives set.

It's important to emphasise that child development is achieved through the method the teacher chooses to follow the stages, with the aim of getting the child to significantly incorporate the importance of play in their learning (RANGEL, 2006).

Paulo Freire (1998, p. 52): "Know that to teach is not to transfer knowledge, but to create possibilities for its own production or its construction." In order to do this, when thinking about teaching, we need to take into account the multiple dimensions that exist within it.

Libâneo (1994) suggests:

> The teacher intentionally uses a set of actions, steps, external conditions and procedures that we call teaching methods to direct and stimulate the teaching process in terms of student learning. For example, the activity of explaining the subject corresponds to the method of exposition, the activity of establishing a conversation or discussion with the class corresponds to the method of joint elaboration. In its meaning, a method leads the teacher to mediate learning actions that make the student understand social reality so that they can be agents of transformation of their reality and understand it, by means of systematised steps that the teacher applies (LIBÂNEO, 1994, p.155).

The same author goes on to emphasise this aspect by saying that the cognitive relationship[5] between the student and the school subject is the axis of the teaching process. Therefore, teaching methods consist of school mediation, with a view to activating students' mental powers to assimilate the content.

Rangel (2006) says that the methodology a teacher chooses, whether it is used to teach literacy or not, aims to provide the best training for the individual in the process of acquiring any knowledge. Each methodology leads the student to have a different reaction to learning and to what is taught in class.

The expository methodology is one of the most commonly used by teachers. In it, the teacher spontaneously uses speech, reading texts, consulting dictionaries and books to pass on to the students the content they need to learn (LIBÂNEO, 1994).

There is also the independent work method, which provides students with an individual task in which they can reflect alone on what is being proposed by the teacher. The student ends up questioning problems, discovering issues, reasoning about them and acquiring their own learning habits (RANGEL, 2006).

---

[5] One who has the aptitude to know; one who has the ability to know.

The elaboration method, according to Libâneo (1994), is based on teacher-student interaction. The teacher draws up pertinent questions and stimulates the students' reasoning so that their answers are thought out and articulated with the content, and that they show an understanding of deeds or facts based on their own experience.

There are teaching methods applied to groups. These are developed on the basis of learning principles and processes based on interaction, dialogue and partnership. The aim is to collectively guarantee students a common knowledge base (RANGEL, 2006).

Rangel (2006) also explains the methods of student work plans. This method favours students' interests and choices. It takes into account their stages of schooling and their autonomy. The teacher is then responsible for offering alternatives, monitoring, guiding and assessing.

According to Libâneo (1994), the Montessori method is based on the principle of understanding the child. This is because this understanding is different from that of the adult and is endowed with self-development. It emphasises the use of concrete materials for understanding and applying concepts.

Quizzing is a method that can be used both as a technique associated with independent study and as a complement to any other method. At any of its stages, discussion is a didactic process that helps to establish, evaluate and recover learning (RANGEL, 2006).

Mettrau (2001), in his chapter 11, describes four other methods: 1) Lesson Method: the students study and plan, together with the teachers, the content and how it will be applied. 2) Problem Method: the teacher poses a problem and provides the tools for the students to solve it. 3) Project Method: the students build and develop an object or theme together. 4) Instructional Module: the students' studies are organised into stages of their knowledge, emphasising the need to assess the students' prior knowledge.

The author also explains that regardless of the method to be used by the teacher, this professional must take into account:

a) Suitability for the objectives set for teaching and learning;
b) The nature of the content to be taught and the type of learning to take place;
c) The characteristics of the students, such as their age group, their level of mental development, their level of interest, their learning expectations;
d) The physical conditions and time available.

Necessarily, these aspects mentioned above correspond to any and all methodology applicable in the school context, specifically in Early Childhood Education.

Just as important is for the nursery school teacher to seek out knowledge in the field of educational psychology in order to understand what stimuli are needed to motivate students. The teacher's perception must be focused on the individual characteristics of each of their pupils, which must be respected (METTRAU, 2001).

According to Marcozzi, Dornelles and Rego (1996):

> [...] Teachers need to observe their pupils, especially in activities that reveal how their thinking is being structured, how they perceive and interpret the world around them, selecting the literacy method according to these characteristics (MARCOZZI; DORNELLES; REGO, 1996, p.142).

It can be seen from the authors' ideas that the mediator of the Early Childhood Education stages is held in high esteem when it comes to the psychological foundations of the stimuli needed to motivate students. Broadening their vocabulary and bringing maturity to the literacy process.

The methodologies applied in Early Childhood Education encompass the cognitive areas that involve the acquisition of written language and reading. According to Vygotsky (2007, p. 90) "oral communication is an excellent way of training language and communicative functions. It stimulates verbal activity and conditions the learning of reading and writing".

Only through the application of effective methods can teachers ensure that their students master their reading skills, because "methods are paths built to reach knowledge and encompass the use of different techniques and instruments". (VYGOTSKY, 2007, p. 92).

The application of a specific teaching method, according to Soares (2001), has been a widely studied and debated topic in the field of pedagogy, due to its complexity and many facets. It has different approaches and has been the object of attention of philosophers, psychologists, linguists and, in particular, educators, which is why it is considered an interdisciplinary field of study in which much has been theorised depending on the time and dominant currents.

According to Aranha (1996, p. 143), "Pestalozzi's philosophical current (17461827) stated that teachers should stimulate the child's spontaneous development". In other words, children are not empty of knowledge, they have experience of the world, which is important for their development.

Another great teacher was Decroly (1871-1932), who founded pre-school education. According to Aranha (1996, p. 173), "Decroly realises that while the adult is capable of analysing, separating the whole into parts, the child tends towards global representations of the whole, that is, perceives facts as a whole."

The Decroly Method is based on globalisation, in which the child's attention is fixed on the whole of things, rather than the details of things. He showed that encompassment is an essential phenomenon of the child's soul, and investigated its impact on teaching and school organisation. Realising that education is about stimulating cognitive structures and affective capacities while paying due attention to cultural content (METTRAU, 2001).

Another significant contribution was the constructivist school of Piaget (1896-1980) and the definition of the different stages of development from birth to adolescence. According to Aranha (1996, p. 184) "Piaget investigates human development where this dynamic process presupposes a structure conceived as a totality in equilibrium".

Nowadays, modern thinkers such as Freire (1987) and liberation theory propose approaches to education on lifelong learning. On the other hand, the emergence of non-formal education and andragogy[6] .

There is no ready-made recipe book when it comes to teaching. Teachers must take advantage of opportunities in which children are willing to learn and be alert when there are children in their classroom with any kind of difficulty or disability (KRAMER, 1995).

The teaching methods presented by the aforementioned theorists can be effective, depending on the child's maturity in learning and the teacher's ability to use the best method. From this perspective, it is understood, as Carneiro (1995) states, that children will learn better if the method is attractive, as playfulness is.

2.7 PLAY AS A CONSTRUCTIVIST PROPOSAL

Constructivism, inspired by the ideas of the Swiss Jean Piaget (1896-1980), is a widely accepted theoretical proposal in the field of learning and teaching, as its approach conceives the principle that encompasses the apprehension of knowledge. The scholar came to the conclusion that knowledge is acquired through the individual's involvement with society, i.e. man's interaction with the environment (BECKER, 1992).

Piaget (1971) explains about this interaction:

> The relationship between the subject and its environment consists of a radical interaction, in such a way that consciousness does not begin with knowledge of objects or the subject's activity, but with an undifferentiated state; and it is from this state that two complementary movements derive, one of incorporation of things into the subject, the other of accommodation to the things themselves (PIAGET, 1971, p. 386).

A student of Piaget's, Emilia Ferreiro (5 May 1937), extended the theory of her master/mentor to the field of reading and writing. She concluded that children can become literate on their own, as

---

[6] It is the art or science of guiding adults to learn, according to the definition credited to Malcolm Knowles in the 1970s. The term refers to a concept of adult education, as opposed to pedagogy, which refers to the education of children (from the Greek paidós, child).

long as they are in an environment that stimulates contact with letters and texts. It also established the stages that children go through until they are truly literate. Nowadays, the constructivist approach has been revived with great force, emerging as an epistemological current whose aim is to find out how human beings create knowledge (DUARTE; ROSSI, 2008).

In the words of Ferreiro (1996):

> Children don't need to reach a certain age, nor do they need teachers to start learning. From birth they are already knowledge builders. They pose difficult and abstract problems and try to find answers to them on their own. They are building complex objects of knowledge. And the writing system is one of them (FERREIRO, 1996, p. 48).

The constructivist conception of learning, although it has many variations, says that every child who creates, recreates and constructs knowledge has autonomy in their construction process, taking from their environment the elements that their cognitive structure is capable of assimilating (RIBEIRO, 1999). It can be seen that in the early stages of learning, children have a high degree of curiosity which leads them to associate and symbolise the events around them.

Ribeiro (1999) cites Piaget's constructivist theoretical principles (18961980):

> The child starts from an egocentric position - one that does not yet distinguish the existence of an external world separate from itself - and goes on to form its intelligence through processes of adaptation, assimilation and accommodation, arriving at an interaction with the external world and therefore reducing egocentrism [...] Piaget started from a biological theory about the construction of human knowledge, in other words, from genetic epistemology, and he explains that it is in the sensory stage that the development of the child's intelligence begins. At this stage, knowledge occurs through the child's physical contact with the object (RIBEIRO, 1999, p. 18).

Each phase in which the child progresses is a phase of construction and structuring of thought and the greatest characteristic of this constructivist learning process is the relationship between the individual and the object. Still in Ribeiro's work (1999, p. 07), she emphasises that "in the constructivist approach, we can affirm that the literacy process occurs differently in each child, reaching different levels at different times".

In this approach, for learning to be effective, the child must be the main actor in the teaching and learning process. According to Ribeiro (1999):

> Recreational activities work to this end, as they allow the student to have a highly participative role, and to feel constantly involved in the psychosocial characteristics that show and enhance intrapersonal (with oneself) and interpersonal (with others) communication, so the student is constantly reflecting on and socialising the knowledge they have built up. (RIBEIRO, 1999, p. 7).

The characteristics that underpin the constructivist proposal are based on the preparation of activities in which the child can be completely interested and involved so that they can realise their knowledge through games and play (BECKER, 1992).

Ribeiro (1999) emphasises the importance of the teacher planning the proposed activities in the constructivist model. In constructivist classrooms, different corners of knowledge are considered, with materials available for children to choose from to learn and play. Group activities are prioritised, with the aim of stimulating cooperation and the exchange of knowledge and experiences, in order to encourage students with more difficulties to relate to each other and feel well accepted by everyone.

The author says of this socialisation:

> [...] listening to the child, more than talking, listening to their curiosities, questions, their life stories, their stored memories, their cultural and social life. Enabling communication, cooperation, socialisation, discovery in order to then seek out objects relating to cognitive content (knowledge) procedural content (practice) attitudinal content (values and attitudes)

(RIBEIRO, 1999 p. 9).

It is very important for the teacher to diagnose the entire development process that the student has achieved during the stages of constructivist literacy. Duarte and Rossi (2008) explain that it is therefore not a question of transferring information mechanically, but rather of exciting the student by encouraging their enchantment with their own perception and organisation of thought.

2.8 THE IMPORTANCE OF THE TEACHER IN PLAY ACTIVITIES

The key elements of the play activity can be considered to be the students, the teachers, the learning, the context and the climate. The teachers' reactions to the students' results will lead to new creations and improvements for other activities and themes (DUARTE; ROSSI, 2008).

It's clear that a large part of the child's time in the literacy process is spent at school, and it's up to the teacher to create a literacy environment that stimulates an understanding of written language in a playful, meaningful way and, above all, one that is close to social conventions. From this perspective, the aforementioned authors define the teacher as the mediator of the construction of knowledge to be developed by the student.

According to Curto (2000, p. 92), "The teacher is the active protagonist of their students' learning. In the first place, they decide what should be taught, the content, the materials, the organisation of the work, the activities, etc.". The importance of this professional in the choice and use of play activities can therefore be seen.

There is no doubt that the literacy teacher is the generator of the student's intellectual progress, which will lead them to codify the world in which they live. The importance of the teacher as a mediator is crucial; they need to contextualise the activities, plan teaching situations and intervene in the action with group dynamics. On the other hand, they must evaluate the activities and fulfil the purpose for which they were planned. In order for this to happen correctly, early childhood education professionals must be self-taught, communicative and open to new knowledge (GARCIA, 2003).

Libâneo (1994) emphasises the actions that teachers must be able to carry out:

> The teacher needs to put the child in a position to think, to learn reflexively, to create the conditions and means for students to develop intellectual capacities and skills so that they master methods of study and intellectual work aimed at their autonomy in the learning process and independence of thought, helping students to choose a path in life, to have convictions that guide their options in the face of real life problems and situations (LIBÂNEO, 1994, p. 71).

However, Ribeiro (1999) adds that teachers must be able to diagnose the cognitive stage of their pupils and then propose activities and changes:

> Teachers need to know how each child is diagnosed, the conceptual levels of cognitive development that children bring when they arrive at school or that they will reach at a certain time, how to diagnose the cognitive stage and operative levels that children are at and how to identify them, what linguistic, artistic and intellectual skills they have already achieved and which ones they need to achieve, how to group students after theoretical diagnoses, the theoretical assumptions for psycho-pedagogical intervention, etc. (RIBEIRO, 1999, p. 31).

It is the teacher's duty to continually self-evaluate their practices, because it is their pedagogical actions that will influence the process of maturing in reading and writing. Self-assessment will ensure that the student achieves optimum results in the process of acquiring knowledge (DUARTE; ROSSI, 2008).

Perrenoud (2002) reinforces the issue of teacher planning, saying that their proposals need to be coherent. He also emphasises that it is important for the teacher to propose conscious work, appropriate to each stage of the student's development. The teacher must make the student understand the activities and their objectives in a dynamic and affective way.

The writer Freire (2008) adds that affectivity is an essential part of playfulness. For her, "play takes place in a cultural context, and it is impossible to dissociate affection and cognition, form and content, from human action" (FREIRE, 2008, p. 154). Therefore, play helps in the process of building the individual and has characteristics intrinsic to affectivity.

2.8.1 TEACHER TRAINING

It's true that the demands of everyday activities limit teachers in their search for continuous training that effectively guides their professional performance. Even so, teachers must not forget that they have the non-transferable role of imparting knowledge in a pleasurable way.

At this point, theoretical and practical training are indispensable. According to Libâneo (1994), this training is not an action, but a process:

> [...] professional training is an intentional and organised pedagogical process of theoretical, scientific and technical preparation to competently direct the teaching process [...] The professional training of teachers is carried out in higher education courses. They are made up of a set of disciplines, coordinated and articulated with each other, whose objectives and contents should converge into a theoretical and methodological unity of the course that covers two dimensions: theoretical training identifies, including specific academic training in the subjects that the teacher will specialise in and pedagogical training involving knowledge of Philosophy, History of Education and Pedagogy itself which contributes to the clarification of the educational phenomenon in the social historical context; practical technical training aimed at the specific professional preparation of the subjects, the psychology of education, educational research and others, and all of this in an articulated manner (LIBÂNEO, 1994, p. 27).

One can see from the author's ideas that teacher training is made up of many details, which end up differentiating it from other professions because it involves reflective and humanistic actions. At the same time, this professional must seek, on a daily basis, to reflect on their practices, articulating them with theory.

According to Almeida and Freitas (2011), schools are playing various new roles in today's society. It has become an area of constant change in which the teacher plays a central role. Knowing that they are responsible for changing students' attitudes and thinking, these professionals also need to be prepared for the new and growing challenges of a generation that has never been more technological.

Alongside this, Perrenoud (2002) describes the profile of a teacher as follows:

> [...] the theory of a professional must bring together the skills of someone who develops concepts and implements them; he identifies the problem, presents it, imagines and applies a solution and thus ensures that it is followed up. He doesn't know in advance the problems that will arise in his practice; he has to constantly build it live, sometimes with a lot of stress without having all the data for a clearer decision. This cannot happen without comprehensive knowledge, academic knowledge, specialised knowledge and knowledge from experience. A professional never starts from nothing (PERRENOUD, 2002, p.11).

Reflective teacher training involves passing on very rich and in-depth didactic knowledge to equip them to look at and reflect on reality. It's not about empty knowledge, but about getting the answers you need. According to Perrenoud (2002, p. 27), "[...] the training of good teachers [...] has to do [...] with the training of people who are capable of evolving, of learning according to their experience...".

This aspect becomes a preparation goal for teachers who reflect on their practice, enabling and optimising the creation of observation, analysis and intervention models. Kramer (1995, p. 106) states that "being a teacher consists of favouring the process, initially enabling children to carry out systematic activities, organised in such a way that the different forms of child representation and expression are gradually expanded".

Teachers should not be indifferent to students from socially or culturally disadvantaged backgrounds. On the contrary, they must understand the need to provide a quality learning process as an instrument for social advancement (ALMEIDA; FREITAS, 2011).

Antunes (2005) says that teachers should value the diversity of knowledge that comes from previous experiences, as this makes children feel that they are entering a new world that is less strange and less hostile. Respecting and considering differences, valuing the knowledge students have and creating a school context that is favourable to learning.

According to Ribeiro (1999), teaching everyone involves the teacher reflecting on their practice, discussing and seeking solutions to the problems that emerge in the literacy process. Considering the students' experiences is vital for planning and implementing playful activities that will serve to restructure the new knowledge they will acquire at school.

The RCNEI - Referencial Curricular Nacional da Educação Infantil (1998) says that the teacher must be able to organise a space: 1) In the classrooms, areas for games, arts, make-believe, reading, etc. According to this document, children learn more in smaller, well-divided spaces. In the outdoor area, the following guidelines apply:

> In the outdoor area, play spaces should be created that are alternative and allow children to run, swing, climb, descend and climb different environments, hang, slide, roll, play ball, play with water and sand, hide, etc. (BRASIL, 1998, p. 69).

The Education Guidelines and Bases Law, sanctioned in December 1996, establishes, in Section II, referring to Early Childhood Education, article 31 that "[...] assessment will be carried out by monitoring and recording their development, without the aim of promotion, even for access to primary education.".

Pimenta (1997) makes the following observation about teacher training:

> A professional identity is built on the social meaning of the profession; on the constant revision of the social meanings of the profession, on the revision of traditions. But also in the reaffirmation of culturally established practices that remain significant. Practices that resist innovation because they are full of knowledge that is valid to the needs of reality, the confrontation between theories and practices, the systematic analysis of practices in the light of existing theories, the construction of new theories. It is also constructed by the meaning that each teacher, as an actor and author, gives to teaching in their daily lives, based on their values, their way of situating themselves in the world, their life stories, their representations, their knowledge, their anxieties and their desires (PIMENTA, 1997, apud GOMES, 2009, p. 41).

As such, these professionals are expected to be capable of constant self-evaluation and of maintaining a link between traditional pedagogical practices and those that emerge over time. In addition, teachers are expected to be able to reconcile practice (outside the classroom) and theory (inside the classroom).

For the National Curriculum Framework for Early Childhood Education (1998), educating means favouring guided learning situations that can contribute to the development of children's interpersonal relationship skills. In addition, an affinity to be and to be with others in a basic attitude of acceptance, respect and trust, and children's access to broader knowledge of social and cultural reality. In this sense, caring and educating must go hand in hand, inseparable, thus marking the identity of this stage of education.

Being able to evaluate. This is another requirement raised by the RCNEI (1998), which defines observation and recording as the main assessment tools. This observation can be recorded in writing, audio and/or video recordings, photographs and children's productions throughout the period.

In the same document, assessment is prioritised as "a set of actions that help the teacher reflect on the learning conditions offered and adjust their practice to the needs of the children". It also adds that the teacher must share the results of this assessment so that the child can keep track of their achievements and difficulties.

CHAPTER 3

METHODOLOGICAL FRAMEWORK

3.1 FOCUS

The focus of this study was to verify the use of play as a tool for the teaching-learning process of students, by teachers at Early Childhood Centres.

3.2 TYPE OF RESEARCH

According to Demo (2000), research varies according to its genre. That said, it should be added that no type of research is self-sufficient. In practice, several have been mixed, emphasising one type or another.

Descriptive research was used to describe and analyse the data obtained through field research. In addition, the aim was to collect numerical data on the perception of parents and students regarding play as a teaching-learning tool.

3.3 TIME AND SPACE DELIMITATION

The data was collected in the month of September 2016, a period that was deemed sufficient to carry out a detailed investigation of the data to be collected.

As for the spatial delimitation, it is set in the Early Childhood Education Centre - CEI, in the city of Caldas Novas, Goiás, Brazil, called Centro de Educação Infantil Pequeno Príncipe.

3.4 POPULATION AND SAMPLE

The population includes all the teachers at CEI: Centro de Educação Infantil Pequeno Príncipe and all the students at this institution, as well as their parents.

Only teachers at the Pequeno Príncipe Early Childhood Education Centre who are permanent, either classroom teachers or support staff, were included. Professionals who are only contracted, and not civil servants, were not included in this sample.

All the teachers at the Pequeno Príncipe Early Childhood Education Centre. The pupils were observed during lessons and break times. Parents were invited to take part in the research, but it was not compulsory.

3.6 HYPOTHESIS

The hypothesis is that the teachers at the Early Childhood Education Centres, specifically at the Pequeno Príncipe Early Childhood Education Centre (CEI), have no specific training in the area of play, either as a subject during their undergraduate or postgraduate studies, or as a continuing or refresher training course.

It was also hypothesised that these teachers were not using play with the real aim of teaching, but just to fill the children's time and keep them occupied during their stay at the institution.

3.7 DATA COLLECTION TECHNIQUES AND INSTRUMENTS

This is the phase of the research carried out in order to gather prior information on the field of interest and involves collecting data from various sources (LAKATOS; MARCONI, 2003).

3.7.1 OBSERVATION

According to Gil (2008), observation is a fundamental element of research and can be used in conjunction with other techniques. We intend to use systematic observation, as it uses pre-structured instruments.

An observation was made of the play activities carried out by the teachers and of the children's behaviour in relation to the activity, in order to see if this action had paid off in terms of the students' teaching-learning process. The observation script (APPENDIX D) was used for this purpose

3.7.2 QUESTIONNAIRE

According to Lakatos and Marconi (2003, p. 21), a "questionnaire is a data collection instrument consisting of an ordered series of questions that must be answered in writing and without the presence of the interviewer".

In addition to observing the play activities and the behaviour of the students during this playfulness, data was obtained from the teachers at the Early Childhood Education Centre through the application of a questionnaire containing 13 closed and 13 open questions.

In order to find out how the parents of these students perceive play, a questionnaire was also sent to the parents containing 10 objective and discursive questions.

3.8 PRIMARY AND SECONDARY SOURCES OF INFORMATION

The primary sources of information include the questionnaire applied to the teachers and parents of the Pequeno Príncipe Early Childhood Education Centre, as well as observation of the play activities carried out by the teachers and the behaviour of the students during this playfulness. Secondary sources: books, articles, monographs, theses, texts available on the Internet, databases, newspapers, magazines, films, among others that deal with play in early childhood education.

3.9 HOW THE DATA COLLECTED WILL BE PROCESSED

The data collected through the questionnaire applied to teachers and parents was analysed using graphs and discursively when the question was open-ended. Similarly, the observation data was represented descriptively and in graph form, for better visualisation and understanding.

3.10 ETHICAL CONSIDERATIONS

The interviewees' real names were used because the coordination and management of CEI Pequeno Príncipe authorised it and provided all the names of the professionals who work at the institution. However, the names of the parents and children will be preserved. For this purpose, alphabetical lists have been used.

CHAPTER 4

ANALYTICAL MARK

4.1 OBSERVATIONS MADE

According to the institution's PPP - Political Pedagogical Project (2016), it was created and maintained by the Catholic Church's Pro-Family Social Centre, with its own headquarters, in partnership with the Caldas Novas-GO City Hall, and was named "O Pequeno Príncipe Nursery School" after the son of the donor of the land on which it was built. Its inauguration took place on 18/01/1984, with the participation of the president of the Social Centre, Sister Tereza, the mayor José Onofre de Carvalho and the secretary of education, Silvânia Fernandes e Silva.

The first headmistress to be appointed was Mrs Laci Guimarães, and in 1986 Mrs Yeda Godoy took over as headmistress, after which Mrs Adélia took over for a certain period. Around 1987, Alcirene Maura Moreira Alves ran the Education Centre until 1988, and then, between 1988 and 1989, she was jointly in charge with Maria José Refundini and Celi Rodrigues Coser. In May 1990, Mrs Alcirene Maura Moreira Alves returned to the helm, and has remained at the head of the educational institution to this day (PPP, 2016).

Currently, according to the PPP (2016), given the process of historical and social change in the role of education, the nursery school is working in accordance with LDB No. 9.394/96, which has brought a new vision to its role, no longer as a place of assistance, but as a place where education and care are interconnected, honouring the cognitive, affective and pedagogical aspects of children's development, thus assuming a new nomenclature "Pequeno Príncipe Children's Education Centre".

CEI Pequeno Príncipe has been located at the same address as its inauguration for 35 years, which is Rua 12, Quadra 38, Lote 12, Setor São José, in the municipality of Caldas Novas-GO, where during these years it has increased its initial attendance from 60 children to an average of 92 children, full-time, with an increase in architectural/physical structure and adaptations (ramps, toilets, doors, etc.) to cater for children with disabilities (PPP, 2016).

Until 2012, according to the PP (2016), CEI Pequeno Príncipe catered for both nursery and pre-school, but in view of the legal determination, the guidelines on agreements between Municipal Education Departments and Community Institutions for the provision of Early Childhood Education (MEC-2009), it began to cater only for nursery, essentially referring to children aged 3 months to 4 years.

The city of Caldas Novas currently has 16 CMEIs - Municipal Early Childhood Education Centres and 3 CEIs - Early Childhood Education Centres. The difference between the two types is that the CMEI is the full responsibility of the municipality, while the CEI has an agreement with the town hall and receives help from churches, companies and other organisations.

The management of CEI Pequeno Príncipe said that the school's opening hours are from 6.45am to 7.30am and the closing hours are from 4pm to 5.30pm. In the morning shift there are: 2 cooks, 1 general services assistant and 1 laundress. In the afternoon: 1 cook, 2 general service assistants, 1 laundress and 1 secretary (full time).

Table 1 - Training of the Management Team

NAME	FUNCTION	HABILITATION
Alcirene Maura Moreira	Director	Degree in Geography and Postgraduate Diploma in Educational Management.
Liara Reis Silva	Pedagogical Coordinator	Graduated in Higher Normal Education; Postgraduate in Neuropedagogy and Psychoanalysis; Master's student in Educational Sciences.
Ivone Gonzaga de Rezende do Prado	Secretary	Accounting Technician.

Source: PPP (2016)

Table 1 shows the members of the Little Prince CEI management team, the position they hold and their academic qualifications. It can be seen that only the secretary does not have a degree in education. The other employees are listed in Table 2 below:

Table 2 - Catering and General Services Team

NAME	FUNCTION	HABILITATION
Coracy Machado de Sousa	Catering assistant	2º Grade incomplete
Dinorah das Dores Silva	General Services Assistant/Gatekeeper	1º Grade incomplete
Luzia Divina Martins do Vai	Laundry	Pro-Children
Roseli da Silva Santos	Laundry	Pro-Children
Maria Apolinário de Sousa Rosa	Catering	Elementary School Completed
Marly Ribeiro	General Services Assistant/Gatekeeper	Pro-Children
Vandair Divina Martins Florisbelo	Catering	Pro-Children
Maria Deusanete	General Services Assistant/Gatekeeper	Elementary School Completed

Source: PPP (2016)

There are a total of 27 teachers and support staff who are in direct, daily contact with the students in the classroom. They take turns in the morning and afternoon, so that there is always a Pedagogue (teacher) and 1 or 2 support staff in the classroom. They will be described in more detail in the following section.

4.2 ANALYSING RESEARCH DATA

This section will analyse the data collected during the questionnaire with teachers, parents and the observations made during the field research.

4.2.1 DATA ANALYSIS: TEACHERS

The teachers and support staff are all female, and there are no male employees at CEI Pequeno Príncipe. Seven of them are teachers and another 20 are support staff. Both range in age from 21 to 52. They cater for children from 3 months to 4 years old. There are an average of 15 children in the class and most of them are female.

Table 3 shows how the Early Childhood Education professionals are distributed among the classes. There are six classrooms, ranging from nursery (3 months) to Maternal 2B, which cater for children up to 4 years old.

There are pedagogues who only work one period, morning or afternoon, and others who work full time for 20 or 40 hours. It is noticeable that the afternoon period has more support staff, due to the fact that they serve lunch and give the children a bath before handing them over to their parents.

Table 3 - Distribution of teachers and support per class

CLASS	TIME	PEDAGOGUE (Regent)	Workload	SUPPORT PROFESSIONAL
Nursery 1	Morning	1		1
	Afternoon	1	10h	2
Nursery 2	Morning	1		1
	Afternoon	1	10h	2
Nursery 1A	Morning	1		1
	Afternoon	1	10h	2
Nursery 1B	Morning	1		1
	Afternoon	1	10h	2

Nursery 2A	Morning	1		1
	Afternoon	1	20h	2
Nursery 2B	Morning	1	40h	2
	Afternoon	1	20h	1
2 volunteer helpers (1 in the morning and 1 in the afternoon)				

Source: Personal collection (2017)

As for the pedagogues' training, all of them have a degree in Pedagogy, and all of them have post-graduate degrees in some area of Education, such as: Educational Management, Neuropedagogy and Psychoanalysis, Early Childhood Education, Educational Guidance, Teaching Methods and Techniques in Early Childhood Education. Two of these teachers are studying for a Master's degree in Educational Sciences.

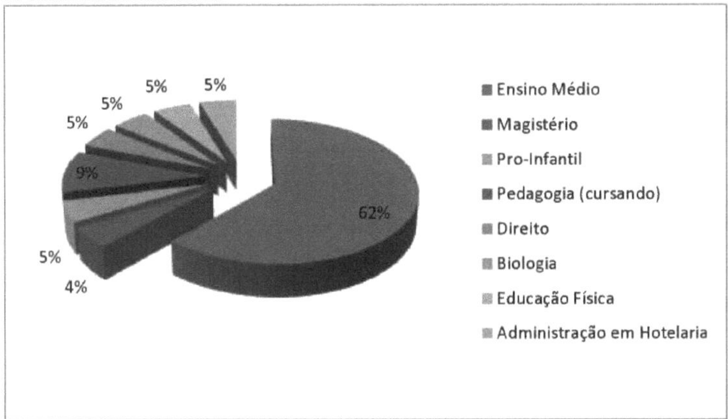

Graph 1 - Training of support professionals
Source: Personal collection (2017)

As for the training of support professionals, Graph 1, on the next page, provides a better breakdown of this training. It's worth remembering that only high school education is required to apply for this position.

It can be seen that 62% of support professionals have only completed secondary school. 9% are studying for a degree in Pedagogy and the rest have degrees in other areas. Some of these fields are quite different from education, such as law and hotel management.

The question arises as to whether this person, who only has a high school degree, has the training to work with early childhood education, especially play. It raises the possibility of a possible discussion on the subject, since these professionals have no specific training in the area.

Question 7 of the questionnaire applied to teachers and support professionals asked "How many times a week do you use play activities to teach your students?". The result is shown in Graph 2:

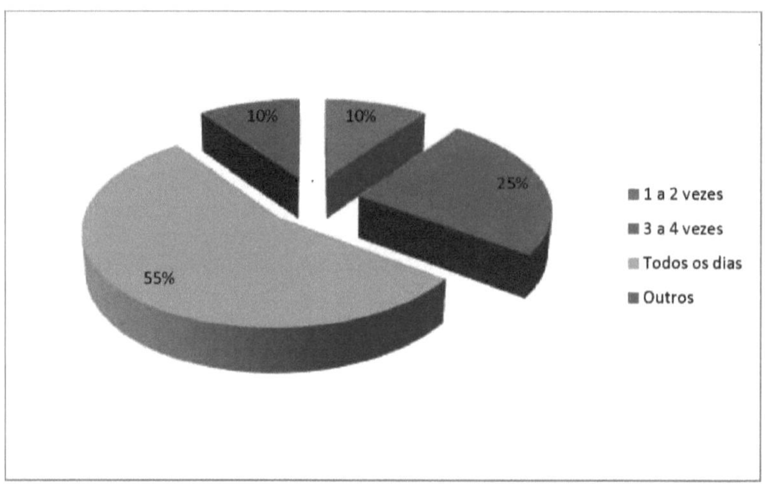

Graph 2 - Number of days using games
Source: Personal collection (2017)

It can be seen that 55 per cent of the teachers said that they use play every day with their students. A further 25% said that they use it 3 to 4 times a day. 10% of those interviewed said that they use play between 1 and 2 times.

Another 10 per cent said they ticked the "Other" box and explained that: "Play is used all the time, to eat, to brush teeth, to bathe and even to sleep." (TEACHER A). Teacher "B" wrote: "We use it when we're going to teach colours, shapes or tell stories, and we do this kind of thing every day at nursery school".

Question 8 asked the teachers and support professionals, "Have you ever taken part in a refresher or training course on play in early childhood education?". The results can be seen in Graph 3 on the next page. 52% of the teachers and professionals said they had already been on a course or training on play. A further 19 per cent said they had not. These 19 per cent refer to newly hired professionals who have recently joined the team.

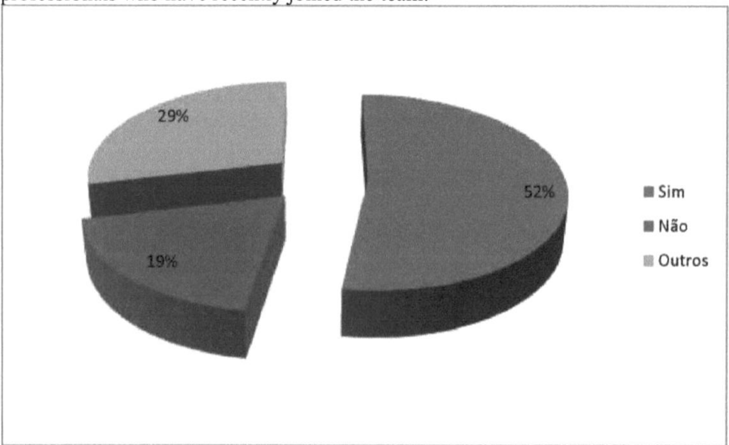

Graph 3 - Professionals who have taken a course on playfulness
Source: Personal collection (2017)

29% of the interviewees ticked "Other" and explained: "We receive training courses throughout the year, but never one specifically on play" (TEACHER B). Teacher "C" explained: "No courses on play, but we have received courses on games and play".

In question 9, teachers and support professionals were asked: "How important do you consider the use of play in the teaching-learning process in Early Childhood Education?". They were given the following options: Extremely Important, Important, Not Very Important and Other.

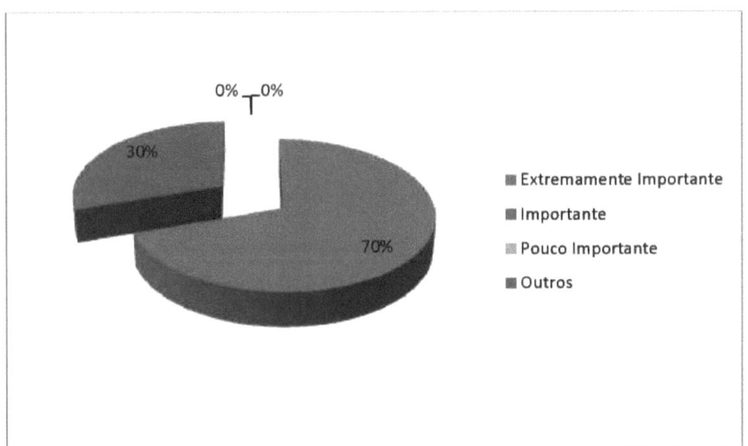

Graph 4 - Importance of play
Source: Personal collection (2017)

Graph 4 shows that the majority of those interviewed answered that they considered play to be "extremely important" for Early Childhood Education, totalling 70%. None of them chose the options "not very important" or "other".

30 per cent of them consider play in early childhood education to be only "important". It's worth noting that all those who chose this option are support professionals and not teaching staff.

Once again, the question arises of the training and qualification of these professionals who, despite the fact that most of them only have secondary education, are responsible for the teaching and learning of nursery school pupils.

I wanted to know which play activities early childhood education professionals use the most to teach their students. As can be seen in Graph 5, the majority, totalling 30%, said that the activity they use most is music.

One of the teachers who chose this option wrote: "Music, of course, because we use music when they arrive, when they go to eat, when they go to sleep, when they brush their teeth and even when they leave". (TEACHER D).

Dance and storytelling were tied on 20 per cent. Teacher "E" wrote: "There's storytelling every day, and we sing and dance too, so I think those are the three most used."

Next in line were 15% for play, 10% for theatre and 5% for games. This low percentage for games is due to the fact that CEI Pequeno Príncipe works with children under the age of 4, who are considered too young to play games.

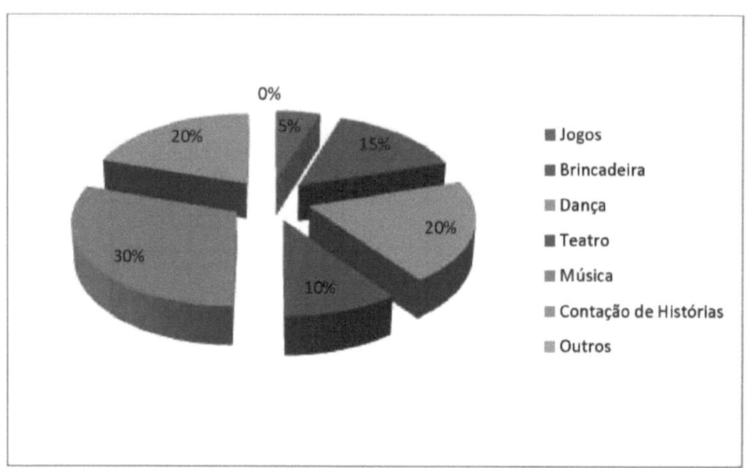

Graph 5 - Most used play activities
Source: Personal collection (2017)

Question 11 asked the professionals: Which of the activities listed in the previous question do you think your students enjoy the most? There were differences of opinion. Most said it was the songs. However, many emphasised that they get very motivated when it's time to tell stories. Question 12 asked whether early childhood education professionals use nursery rhymes and traditional games to teach their pupils. They all said yes.

The majority gave as an example nursery rhymes such as: Atirei o pau no gato; Cabra cega; Bata quente; Ciranda cirandinha; Corre cotia and so on. Other teachers said they use games such as: Bambolê; Amarelinha; Cobrinha; Pula corda; Dança da cadeira; Esconde-esconde; estátua; João bobo; Morto-vivo; Peteca; Pega-pega; Seu lobo and even kite.

Graph 6 shows that 60 per cent of children, according to the teachers, prefer electronic games, while 40 per cent prefer educational games.

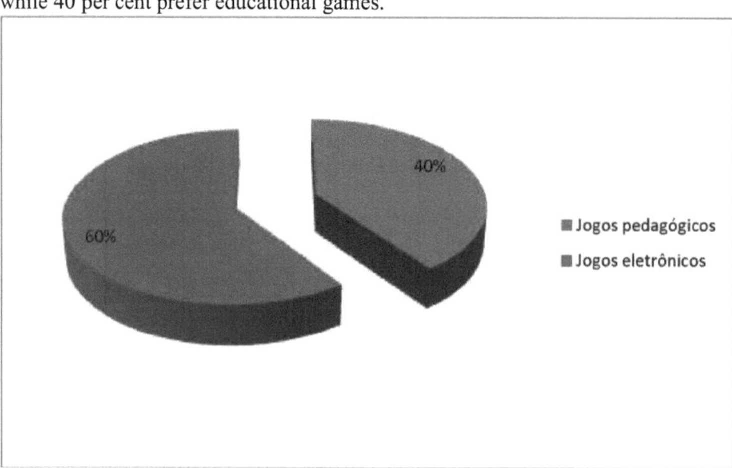

Graph 6 - What children prefer
Source: Personal collection (2017)

Question 14 asked: "Which educational toy do you use the most in the classroom and does it teach your pupils?".

Teachers gave a wide range of answers: puzzles; building games; colourful block games; geometric shape games.

All the teachers agreed that it is very important for parents to encourage play activities at home, because, according to one of the teachers: "If they dedicated this time to their children, our work here would be easier, but they don't do it".

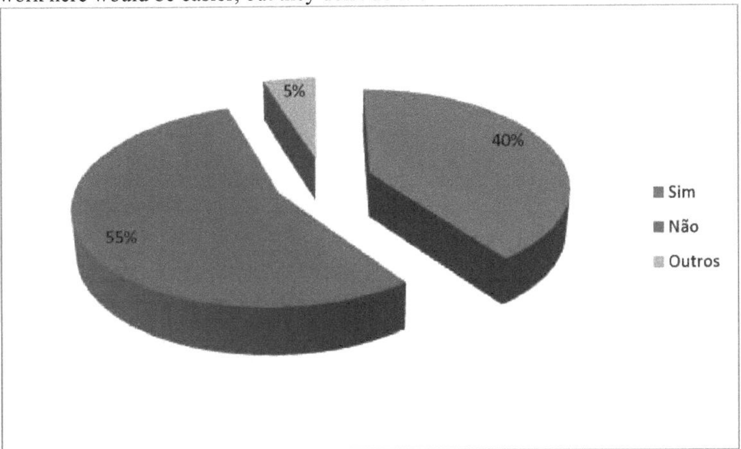

Graph 7 - Parents encourage play at home
Source: Personal collection (2017)

We then sought to find out from teachers and support professionals "Do you realise that your students' parents encourage them to play games that don't involve media and technology?", in question number 15.

Graph 7 on the previous page shows that the majority of teachers believe that parents don't encourage play at home with their children. Another 40 per cent believe that parents encourage their children to play instead of using electronic equipment.

5% of the teachers and support professionals chose the option "Other". Two of the teachers explained that "Parents generally work a lot and don't spend time with their children at home" (TEACHER E).

Another teacher, listed here as Teacher F, described today's world as very technological. Everyone is extremely and increasingly connected to their mobile phones. She also said that children are born knowing how to use a mobile phone and that by the age of 2 or 4 they can even "read" or handle these electronic devices perfectly. She concludes that "[...] it would be impossible for parents to offer something to their children that they themselves don't value."

Question 17 asked the following question: "Does the play activity provide educational accessibility, due to the fact that students are different and because there are students with disabilities in the classroom?". The data is shown in Graph 8.

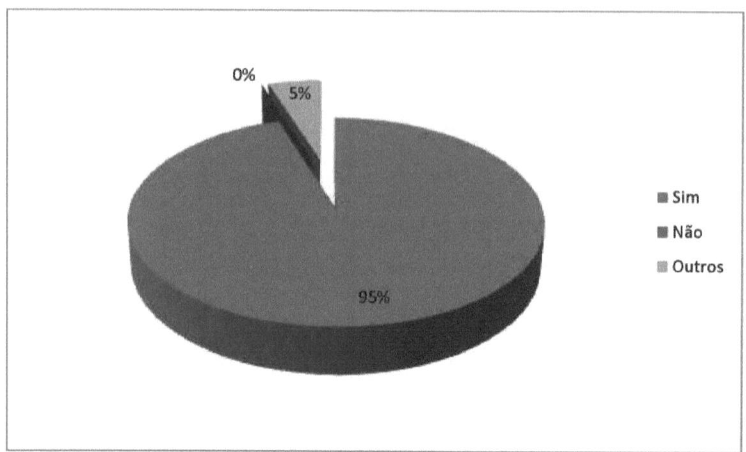

Graph 8 - Play provides educational accessibility
Source: Personal collection (2017)

95 per cent of teachers and support professionals said "yes", play brings educational accessibility, especially for children with disabilities.

One of the teachers answered "Other" and justified it as follows:

> I think that play activities make students feel more equal. In our environment, there are children with parents who have more or less money. Those from more financially controlled families generally learn faster or come from home knowing colours and numbers. The others don't. So I think that play makes everyone learn at the same level. (TEACHER G)

We can see that the teacher has a very broad vision of what play is and the advantages it can bring to early childhood education.

They also wanted to know who participates more in play activities, boys or girls. The result, as shown in Graph 9, is that girls participate more in play, according to the teachers.

One of the teachers, even though she had ticked the "Girls" box, decided to leave her justification and wrote:

> I've been working in this institution for over 10 years and I can say that everyone takes part in the games that are chosen without emphasising gender (male or female). It used to be that the boys were more reluctant to sing and dance, but today I can say that this is no longer the case. I believe that the girls are more uninhibited and in greater numbers, which is why they seem to be the most participative. (TEACHER H).

It can therefore be inferred that because the number of girls at CEI Pequeno Príncipe is higher, they end up taking part in more play activities.

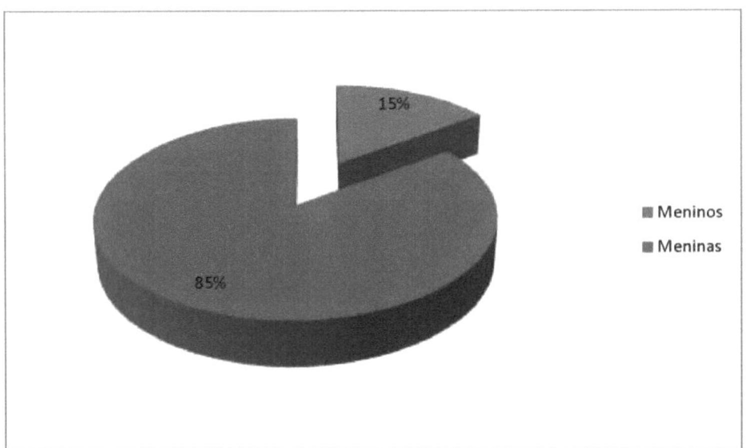

Graph 9 - Who participates most in play activities
Source: Personal collection (2017)

Question 19 asked "Does the CMEI where you work encourage the use of playful pedagogical practices?".

Graph 10 shows that 75 per cent of teachers say that CEI Pequeno Príncipe encourages the use of play. 15% answered "sometimes" and a further 10% ticked the "Other" box. Of the teachers who ticked "sometimes", they left their justification, which is transcribed below:

> I don't think it always encourages it. We do it because we know it's the right thing to do. We were taught to work like this when we studied for Early Childhood Education. But I can't say that someone from the school office makes us use play or encourages us to use it. (TEACHER D).

There is therefore a discrepancy in the teacher's statement that there is no incentive or demand from the CEI's management regarding the use of play in the classroom.

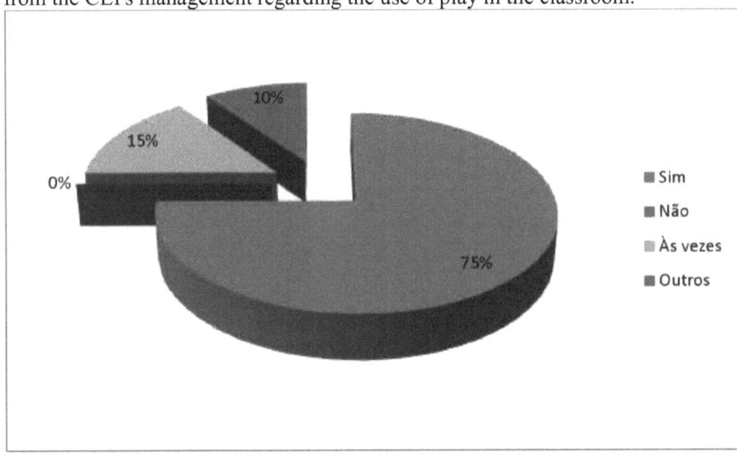

Graph 10 - CEI Pequeno Príncipe encourages the use of play
Source: Personal collection (2017)

Question 20 asked "What results do you get from playfulness?". The options to be ticked by teachers and support professionals were: Increased student motivation; Greater participation in

activities; Memorisation of what was taught; More efficient learning and Other.
The results of this question can be seen in Graph 11 below:

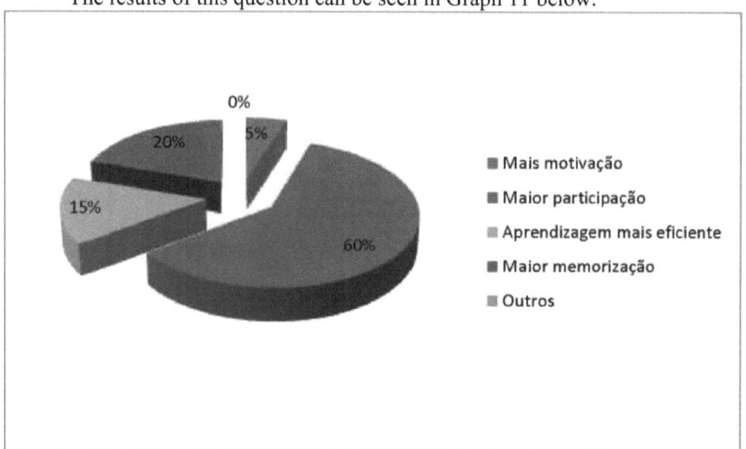

Graph 11 - Results of the use of playfulness
Source: Personal collection (2017)

The majority, totalling 60% of teachers and support professionals, believe that when playfulness is used, the result is greater student participation in activities.

Another 20% believe that students end up memorising more of what they are taught. And 15 per cent believe that learning becomes more efficient. 5% replied that students are more motivated to take part in play activities.

In question 21, the teachers and support professionals at CEI Pequeno Príncipe were asked: "When does the use of play become a valuable activity?". Most answered that it is when the student is able to learn in a pleasurable way.

In question 22, the participants were asked: "Do you think that reading can also have a playful value? How?". Unanimously, the teachers answered "Yes" and among the justifications, Teacher I's stands out: "Yes, because the story in Early Childhood Education, for this age, is not just reading, we have to dramatise, act out, make the voices and gestures of the characters".

Question 23 asked: "How is learning involving play assessed?". According to the interviewees, assessment is daily. Teacher J's response stands out:

> "We make a report on the students when they arrive in our classrooms. Then we analyse and note down each development. It's possible, during a game, for me to realise if my pupil has improved their motor coordination, for example." (TEACHER J).

The teachers were asked about the importance of using play in learning. The majority answered, in agreement with question 21, that it is "The student learns by playing".

We also asked about the difficulties faced by early childhood teachers in working with playfulness in the classroom. Some of them stand out: "The classroom is too full", "Lack of quality teaching materials", "The very young age of the pupils", "The routine in the classroom".

To conclude, the teachers were asked the following question: "In your opinion, what play activities are capable of contributing to the child's maturation in literacy? Give examples. The five most frequently cited stand out: "Games with the letters of the alphabet", "Songs with numbers", "Playing with colours", "Storytelling that works on students' (oral) interpretation", "Pedagogical objects that work on sums".

A questionnaire (APPENDIX C) with 7 objective questions and 3 discursive questions was also administered to the students' parents.

On 5 September 2016, all the students at CEI Pequeno Príncipe took the questionnaire home to complete and hand it in by 9 September. So 87 questionnaires were distributed and 63 questionnaires were returned by parents or guardians.

The first question asked parents if they thought it was important for their child to play. All the parents answered "Yes". None of them answered "No" and none of them justified their answer.

The second question asked: "Do you believe that children learn through play?". The answers were unanimous, as all the parents said "Yes". One parent argued: "If the play is well directed, they learn a lot".

The third question asked parents which educational toys their child has at home. Graph 12 lists the most frequently mentioned toys.

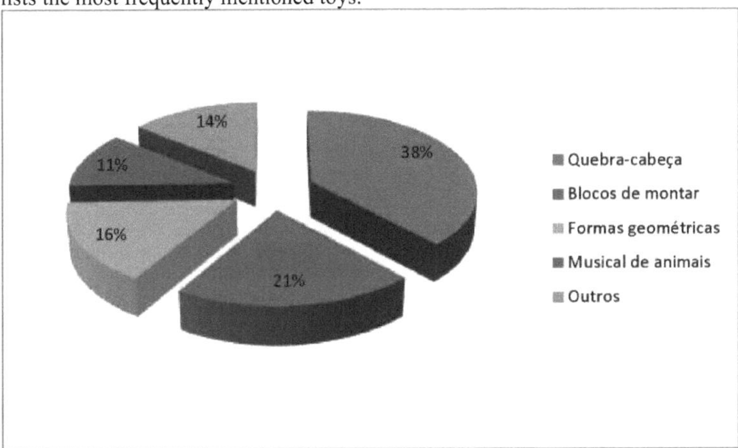

Graph 12 - Educational toys at home
Source: Personal collection (2017)

It can be seen that puzzles are the toy that children have most often at home, with 38 per cent. This was followed by 21% of building blocks and 16% of geometric shapes. 11% of parents said that their children have musical toys with animal sounds. Another 14% mentioned other toys such as "Piano with colours", "EVA alphabet" and "Pot with numbers".

In question 4, parents were asked: "Do you know what play is?". Graph 13 shows the results of the survey.

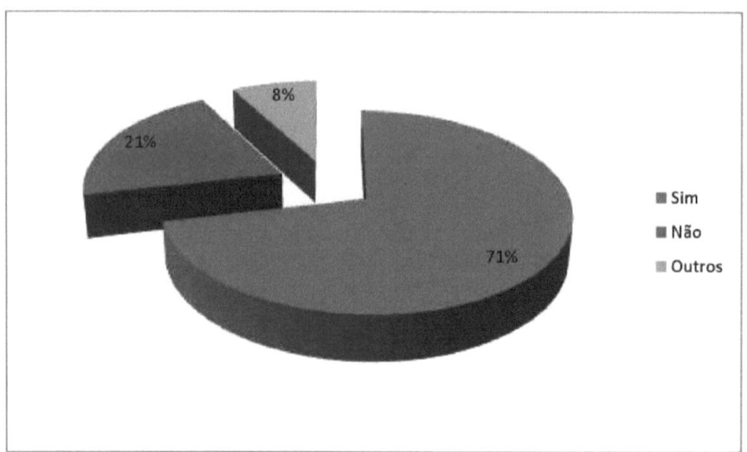

Graph 13 - Parents who know what play is
Source: Personal collection (2017)

It can be seen that 71 per cent of parents replied that they knew what play was. A further 21 per cent said they didn't know what it was and 8 per cent ticked the "Other" box and explained that they didn't know what it was, but had looked it up on the internet at the time.

In question 5, I wanted to find out from the parents of students at CEI Pequeno Príncipe whether they encourage their children to have fun with games that don't involve media and technology.

All the parents answered "YES". Two of them left a justification that is transcribed here: "I try, but at almost four years old he loves playing on the tablet", another father wrote "I buy lots of toys and educational games, but he really likes electronic things, I think he keeps up with his older brother".

Question 6 asked parents: "Which one do you think your child would choose?".

The results are compiled in Graph 14 and show that the majority of parents believe that their children prefer electronic games to educational games

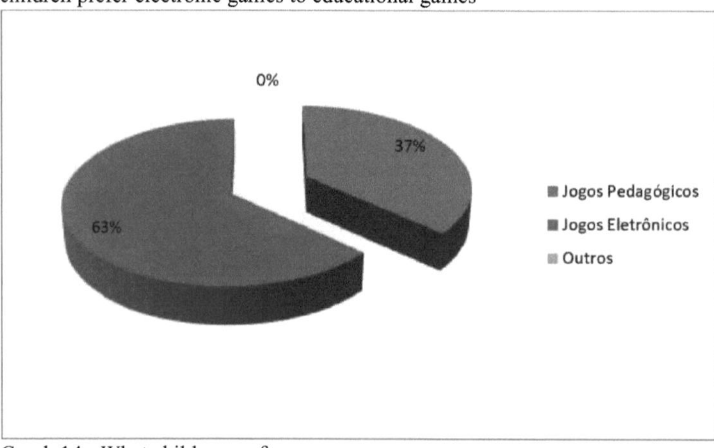

Graph 14 - What children prefer
Source: Personal collection (2017)

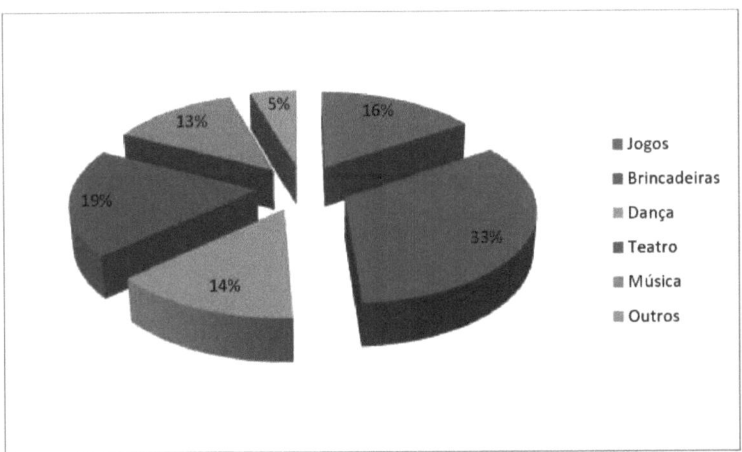

Graph 15 - Parents believe that teachers use more
Source: Personal collection (2017)

Parents were asked if they knew which play activity is most used by CEI Pequeno Príncipe. The following options were given: Games, Play, Dance, Theatre, Music and Other.

This question was asked in order to understand whether parents are aware of what happens in their child's day-to-day life, whether they are participative and aware of the pedagogical practices used by teachers.

Graph 15, on the previous page, compiles the data collected from this question, which is listed as question 7 of the questionnaire applied to the parents of students at CEI Pequeno Príncipe.

It can be seen that parents believe that CEI teachers use play more to work with children, as shown in Graph 15, with 33%. This was followed by theatre with 19%, then games with 16% and dance with 14%. Music followed with 13% and 4% ticked the "Other" box.

Question 8 asked parents which games they enjoyed as children and which they taught their child. Several items were mentioned, four of which stood out: "Cirandinha", "Bolinha de sabão", "Esconde-esconde" and "Batata quente".

Question 9 asked: "Apart from having fun, what else do you believe that games and nursery rhymes can offer your child?". There were several answers with different arguments, but they all emphasised the issue of learning and quality time dedicated to the child.

Finally, the parents were asked: "Do you think it's important for nursery school teachers to study play (games, games, nursery rhymes, storytelling, etc.)?". Parents unanimously answered "yes", they believe that teachers should be trained in this area. One of the parents explained: "I think that every kindergarten teacher should be prepared to work with these playful things in the classroom, because that's how the little ones learn".

4.1.2 DATA ANALYSIS: OBSERVATION

In addition to the questionnaire applied to teachers and the questionnaire applied to parents, an observation was drawn up with 14 items to be evaluated (APPENDIX D).

The observation took place in September 2016, on the following days: 01 and 02; 12 and 13; 21, 22 and 30. Different days of the week were chosen so that it would be possible to follow the CEI's routine and be in a different classroom each day.

During this period it was possible to follow each group of teachers from the moment they received the students until the moment they left. Observation thus provided a complement to the research that will be described in this section.

It was possible to observe that the teacher uses playful activities on a daily basis, in the classroom and outside it, such as at snack time and when brushing teeth. Most of the students take part in the activities and are happy and excited to be part of them. Some didn't want to take part because they were shy, sick or sleepy.

It was also noted that traditional games, songs and plays are present in the daily life of CEI Pequeno Príncipe, but not every day. We realised that on days after the activities, the students are able to remember the game or the songs. Some even ask to "sing it again", for example.

It was not possible to ascertain whether there is a change in the children's behaviour or attitude after they have been taught something through play. Similarly, it was not possible to ascertain whether the students understood the educational meaning of the game. To this end, it is felt that the observation time should have been longer.

The teacher at CEI Pequeno Príncipe plans the play activities in a specific notebook and presents it to the pedagogical coordinator every fortnight. It was possible to notice a concern on the part of the teachers and support staff to teach through play, but it was not possible to ascertain the same concern on the part of the management and coordination.

It was observed that the teaching-learning process becomes more enjoyable with the inclusion of playful activities as pedagogical practices. The teachers, for the most part, showed affection during the playful activities. However, some lacked enthusiasm, as they seemed to sing or play just for the sake of it.

As for assessment through play activities, it was not possible to see it being used. During the observation period, none of the teachers wrote down, reported or listed any kind of diagnosis regarding the students' progress or learning.

CHAPTER 5

CONCLUSION

5.1 FINAL CONSIDERATIONS

Working with early childhood education is very delicate because it is the beginning of children's education and lives. At this stage we are looking for much more than just the application of content. Little ones need to be prepared for countless life situations and it's the school's responsibility to ensure that these little beings enter the educational journey.

As the National Curriculum Framework for Early Childhood Education (1998) states, play should be a constant element in children's daily school life. However, these playful activities need to be seen as an instrument that contributes to learning, and are no longer just used during breaks in pedagogical activities or as a way of filling in the daily planning and completing the workload.

Playful activities are important in the process of development and learning, especially in the sensory-motor and pre-operative stages, periods in which children are at school level. In their research, scholars such as Vygotsky and Piaget have already emphasised the importance of playful activities, be they assembly games, make-believe games, symbolic games, rule games or free play for children.

Playfulness is a natural part of children's lives, because when they play they work on their physical, motor, emotional, social and cognitive skills. This makes playful activities an important element in the development and learning process. As such, it can be emphasised that play has a significant dimension to be explored by professionals working in Early Childhood Education.

Based on the bibliographical research, the application of questionnaires to parents and teachers and the observation carried out at the Pequeno Príncipe CEI in Caldas Novas, Goiás, it was realised that the teachers and support staff understand play and consciously use play-based activities at various times in their routine.

According to the teachers and the results observed, the use of playful activities leads to better performance and involvement by the children in the activities carried out. When activities are used without playful support, a greater effort is needed to get the students' attention and to obtain feedback on the content they wanted to work on. It is worth emphasising that the learning provided by play does not only happen when it is combined with educational activities, but also when children play freely.

It is understood that the Pequeno Príncipe CEI, by encouraging and demanding planning of daily activities, stimulates the teachers' creativity and facilitates their actions and the children's enjoyment. In this way, it is understood that these professionals make a prior and subsequent diagnosis of their class, so as not to run the risk of using play without a goal and purpose.

It is understood that it is important for early childhood education professionals to be prepared, both teachers and support professionals, so that there is no plastering of pedagogical activities. The level of intellectual, physical and emotional development of the children must therefore be taken into account.

At the beginning of this work, we hypothesised that the teachers at CEI Pequeno Príncipe had specific training in the area of play. This hypothesis was proven. Both teachers are pedagogues and studied play as part of their Teaching Practice, not as a subject in their degree programme. As for continuing or refresher training courses on play, some said they had done so and others had not.

It was also hypothesised that these teachers were not using play with the real aim of teaching, but just to fill the children's time and keep them occupied during their stay at the institution. This hypothesis was not possible to prove, as the observation time would have had to be longer to ascertain the teachers' intentionality in this area.

At the beginning of this study, the aim was to find out how teachers at Early Childhood Centres use play as a tool in the teaching-learning process. It was possible to prove that teachers use play and consider it important for this educational stage.

The perception that teachers and students have of playful pedagogical practices was investigated. The teachers recognise its importance and use it on a daily basis, and the students meet the teachers' expectations by participating and learning.

This study is not intended to finalise the subject. The aim of this research, in demonstrating a universe where playfulness is used, was to point to playfulness as an alternative for the methodology used in Early Childhood Education, not as a single resource, but as a strategy that does not preclude the simultaneous use of other resources and methodological strategies. It is hoped that professionals in this area will understand the importance of this strategy and realise how it can be a great ally in their work.

5.2 RECOMMENDATIONS

To finalise this work, here are some recommendations that are considered important for the successful use of play in Early Childhood Education.

5.2.1 To Early Childhood Education professionals

As mentioned in the Theoretical Framework for this research, the Law of Guidelines and Bases 9.394/96 states that assessment should be carried out by monitoring and recording the child's development. The RCNEI (1998) defines observation and recording as the main assessment tools. Duarte and Rossi (2008) add that self-evaluation should be a continuous practice. It should be used to reflect on the learning conditions offered and adjust their practices to the needs of the students.

This is because, during the observation, it wasn't possible to see any notes or records made by the teachers for ongoing student assessment or self-assessment of their own work. The recommendation here is that teachers and classroom managers make more use of this resource.

Like Perrenoud (2002), planning must contain coherent and consistent proposals. Students must be made to understand the activities and their pre-established objectives in a dynamic and affective way. However, in order to know if the objectives have been achieved, the students and their own work must be continually assessed.

5.2.2 To the parents of the students at CEI Pequeno Príncipe

Because it was noted in the field research that children prefer electronic games - this was said by both teachers and parents. Parents said that it was difficult to get children away from electronic equipment and that they didn't have time to teach their children to play.

We recommend that parents encourage their children to play more. Use more educational toys and include storytelling in their children's daily lives. Parents are also advised to dedicate quality time to play activities with their children, so that they can be active participants in their children's teaching and learning process.

As Nascimento (2012) says in the Theoretical Framework, learning is enriched by the dynamic and virtual space of online games. However, parents must realise, as Kishimoto (1993) mentions, that by passing on their knowledge to their children, they are offering them meaningful learning.

It is understood that a lack of space or time to play can lead to possible developmental disorders. It is through playing that children develop their creative spirit and sharpen their intellectual, physical and psychological capacities.

5.2.3 To CEI Pequeno Príncipe

It is recommended that CEI Pequeno Príncipe offer its support staff specific training on playfulness in early childhood education. This is because it was realised that most of them have only completed medical school and are not prepared to be in the classroom applying a pedagogical practice that they themselves do not understand.

It was not possible to ascertain whether there is any encouragement from the management and pedagogical coordination to use play in the classroom. However, it is recommended that both management and coordination work together with teacher educators and other Early Childhood Education professionals. This is to encourage the use of play as a tool for learning and teacher self-assessment.

There was a discrepancy in the answers given by teachers and parents regarding the activities most used at the Centre. The teachers said they used music the most and the parents said they used games the most. It is therefore understood that parents are not aware of the methodologies used by education professionals. It is therefore recommended that the coordination and management of CEI Pequeno Príncipe provide parents with more information about their teaching methodologies.

BIBLIOGRAPHICAL REFERENCES

ABBRI - **Associação Brasileira de Brinquedotecas.** undated. Available at: <http://brinquedoteca.net.br/?p=1747>. Accessed on 19 October 2016.

ALMEIDA, Anne. **Playfulness as a** **pedagogical tool**. 2006. Available at: http://www.cdof.com.br/recrea22.htm. Accessed on 07 September 2016.

ALMEIDA, Marcus Garcia de; FREITAS, Maria do Carmo Duarte. **The School of the 21st Century. The** Actors Responsible for Education and Their Roles. São Paulo: Brasport, 2011.

ALMEIDA, Paulo Nunes de. **Educação Lúdica:** técnicas e jogos pedagógicos. São Paulo: Loyola, 1995.

ANTUNES, C. **Jogos para a estimulação das múltiplas intelligências:** os jogos e os parâmetros curriculares nacionais. Campinas: Papirus, 2005.

ARANHA, M. L. **História da Educação.** 2. ed. rev. São Paulo: Moderna, 1996.

BALDUS, H. **Bibliografia crítica da Etnologia Brasileira**. v. I., Nendeln Liechtenstein: Kraus Reprint, 1970.

BECKER, Fernando. **What is constructivism?** Revista de Educação AEC, Brasília, v. 21, n.83, p. 7-15, Apr./Jun. 1992.

BENJAMIN, W. **One-way street.** São Paulo: Brasiliense, 2002.

BERGEN, Doris. **The Role of Pretend Play in Children's Cognitive Development** 2002. Available at: <http://ecrp.uiuc.edu/v4n1/bergen.html>. Accessed on 07 September 2016.

BRAZIL. Constitution (1988). **Constitution of the Federative Republic of Brazil.** Organised by Alexandre de Moraes. 16.ed. São Paulo: Atlas, 2000.

______ . Ministry of Education and Sports. Secretariat for Basic Education. **Referencial Curricular Nacional para a Educação Infantil/** - Brasília: MEC/SEF, 1998.

. **Statute of the Child and Adolescent:** Federal Law No. 8069, of 13 July 1990. Rio de Janeiro: Official Press, 2002.

______ . Ministry of Education and Sports. Secretariat for Basic Education. **National early childhood education policy.** Brasília, DF: MEC/SEB, 2006.

CARNEIRO, M. A. B. **Aprendendo através da brincadeira.** Ande, Revista da Associação Nacional de Educação, ao 13, n° 21, Cortez Editores, 1995.

CASTELLS, Manuel. **The Internet Galaxy:** Reflections on the Internet, Business and Society. Trad. Maria Luiza X. de A. Borges. Rio de Janeiro: Jorge Zahar, 2006.

CSIKSZENTMIHALY, Mihaly. Living Well. London: Phoenix, 1997.

CURTO, Luiz Mruny et al. (eds.) - **How children learn and how teachers can teach them to write and read.** Vol. 2. ed. Porto Alegre: Medicas Sul, 2000.

DEMO, Pedro. **Methodology of scientific knowledge**. São Paulo: Atlas, 2000.

DIDONET, Vital. Crèche: where it came from, where it's going. In: **Early Childhood Education**: the crèche, a good start. Em Aberto/Instituto Nacional de Estudos e Pesquisas Educacionais. v 18, n.73. Brasília, 2001. p.11-28.

DUARTE, Karina; ROSSI, Karla. **The child's literacy process according to Emilia Ferreiro.** Electronic Scientific Journal of Pedagogy - ISSN: 1678-300X. Year VI. Number 11. January 2008.

FERREIRA, Aurélio B. de Hollanda. **New Dictionary of the Portuguese Language.** 2. ed. Rio de Janeiro: GNT, 2000.

FERREIRO, Emilia. **Literacy in Process.** São Paulo: Cortez, 1996.

FISCHINGER, Bárbara Sybille. **Considerations on Cerebral Palsy and Its Treatment.** Porto Alegre: Sulina Edition, 1970.

FREIRE, Ivete de Aquino. Play, Movement and Dialogue. In: BRASILEIRO, Suely A.; AMARAL, Nair F. Gurgel do; VERLANGA, Carmem Tereza (eds) **Reflexões e Sugestões Práticas para Atuação da Educação Infantil.** Campinas/SP: Alínea, 2008.

FREIRE, Paulo. **Pedagogy of the Oppressed.** 17. ed. Rio de Janeiro: Paz e Terra, 1987.

_______ . FREIRE, Paulo. **Education in the city.** São Paulo: Cortez, 1998.

GARCIA, Regina Leite et al. (eds.) **A formação da professora alfabetizadora, reflexões sobre a prática.** 4. ed. São Paulo: Cortez, 2003.

GIL, A. C. **Como elaborar projetos de pesquisa.** 4. ed. São Paulo: Atlas, 2008.

GOMES, Marineide de Oliveira. **Teacher training in early childhood education.** São Paulo: Cortez, 2009.

KISCHIMOTO, T. M. **Jogos tradicionais Infantis:** O jogo, a Criança e a Educação. Petrópolis: Vozes, 1993.

_______ . **Playroom.** Play space stimulates creativity and socialisation. AMAE EDUCANDO, n. 250, p. 13-15, 1995.

KRAMER, Sônia. Literacy reading and writing. In: **Teacher training in progress.** Rio de Janeiro: Ed. Papéis e Cópias da Escola de Professores, 1995.

LAJOLO, M.; ZILBERMAN, R. **Literatura infantil brasileira.** 6. ed. São Paulo: Ática, 1999.

LAKATOS, E. M.; MARCONI, M. A. **Fundamentos de metodologia científica.** 5. ed. São Paulo: Atlas, 2003.

LIBÂNEO, José Carlos. **Didática.** (Coleção Magistério. 2° grau. Série formação do professor). São Paulo: Ed. Cortez, 1994.

LOPES, Vanessa Gomes. **Language of the Body and Movement.** Curitiba/PR: FAEL, 2006.

MACEDO, L.; PETTY, A. L.; PASSOS, N. C. **Os jogos e o lúdico na aprendizagem escolar.** Porto Alegre: Editora Artmed, 2005.

MACHADO, Rejane Flor; FRISON, Lourdes Maria Bragagnolo. **Self-regulation of learning.** 2012. Available at: <https://periodicos.ufpel.edu.br/ojs2/index.php/caduc/article/view/2153/1970>. Accessed on 10 October 2016.

MARCOZZI, Alayde Madeira; DORNELLES, Leny Werneck; REGO, Marion Vilas Boas de Sá. **Teaching the Child.** 3. ed. Rio de Janeiro: Ao livro técnico, 1996.

METTRAU, M. B. (org.) **Intelligence:** Social Heritage. Rio de Janeiro: Quality Market, 2001.

NASCIMENTO, José Silva do. **The Insertion of Technologies in Playful and Recreational Activities in Classes of 4th and 5th Years of Elementary School Early Years.** Pro-Licenciatura Programme at the University of Brasília, 2012.

NASIO, J.D. **Introduction to the works of Freud, Ferenczi, Groddeck, Klein, Winnicott, Dolto, Lacan.** Translated by Vera Ribeiro. Rio de Janeiro: Jorge Zahar, 1995, p. 194.

NOVAES, J. C . **Playing on Wheels.** Rio de Janeiro: Agir, 1992.

OLIVEIRA, Paulo de Salles. **O que é Brinquedo**. 2. ed. São Paulo: Brasiliense, 1989.

PERRENOUD, Philippe. **Reflective practice in the teaching profession, professionalisation and pedagogical reason.** Translated by Cláudia Schilling. Cláudia Schilling. Porto Alegre: Ed. Artmed, 2002.

PIAGET, J. **Birth of intelligence in the child.** São Paulo: Zahar, 1971

_____ . **Learning and knowledge.** Rio de Janeiro: Freitas Bastos, 1975.

_____ . **The Formation of the Symbol in the Child:** Imitation, Play and Dream. Rio de Janeiro: Zanar, 1978.

PPP. **Pedagogical Political Project.** Pequeno Príncipe Early Childhood Education Centre. 2016.

RANGEL, Mary. **Teaching methods for learning and making lessons more dynamic.** Campinas, SP: Papirus, 2006.

RIBEIRO, Lurdes Eustáquio Pinto. Didactic Proposals for Literacy. In: **A prática construtivista.** São Paulo: Ed. Didática Paulista, 1999.

RODRIGUES, Edvânia Braz T. (org). **Storytelling in the School Space:** contemporary challenges and possibilities. Goiânia: Seduc-GO, 2009.

RONCA, P. A. C. A **aula operatória e a construção do conhecimento.** São Paulo: Edisplan, 1989.

PIAGET, J. **A formação do símbolo na criança:** imitação, jogo e sonho, imagem e representação. Rio de Janeiro: Zahar/INL, 1975.

SANTOS, Santa Marli Pires dos (org.). **Brinquedoteca:** o lúdico em diferentes contextos. Petrópolis/RJ: Vozes, 1997.

SNEYDERS, Georges. **Happy Students.** São Paulo: Paz e Terra, 1996.

SOARES, M. H. F. B. **Jogos e Atividades Lúdicas:** Teoria, Métodos e Aplicações Curitiba/PR: UFPR, 2001.

VIEIRA, Isabel Maria de Carvalho. **The role of fairy tales in the construction of children's imagination.** In: Revista criança - do professor de educação infantil, v. 38, p. 10, 2005.

VYGOTSKY, L. **The Social Formation of the Mind.** 7. ed. São Paulo: Martins Fontes, 2007.

WINNICOTT, D. W. **Play and reality.** Rio de Janeiro: Imago, 1995.

I want morebooks!

Buy your books fast and straightforward online - at one of world's fastest growing online book stores! Environmentally sound due to Print-on-Demand technologies.

Buy your books online at
www.morebooks.shop

Kaufen Sie Ihre Bücher schnell und unkompliziert online – auf einer der am schnellsten wachsenden Buchhandelsplattformen weltweit! Dank Print-On-Demand umwelt- und ressourcenschonend produziert.

Bücher schneller online kaufen
www.morebooks.shop

info@omniscriptum.com
www.omniscriptum.com

MIX
Papier aus verantwortungsvollen Quellen
Paper from responsible sources
FSC® C105338
FSC
www.fsc.org

Printed by Books on Demand GmbH, Norderstedt / Germany